D0725597

Stories
around the Table

... ~ ...

Laughter, Wisdom, and Strength
in Military Life

Elva Resa * Saint Paul

Stories Around the Table: Laughter, Wisdom, and Strength in Military Life
© 2014 Elva Resa Publishing

Individual essays copyright of respective authors.

Cover photo © 2014 Karen Pavlicin-Fragnito. A special thank you to Jeff Ross of Ross Pictures for conducting the cover photo shoot, and to cover models Elsa Bardwell, Ryan Bird, David Edgerton, Michelle Edgerton, Naomi Edgerton, Ciana Fragnito, Elizabeth Hjort, and Alexander Pavlicin.

Compiled and edited by Terri Barnes for Elva Resa.
Design by Andermax Studios and Connie DeFlorin.

The Library of Congress has catalogued this work under LCCN: 2014033460.

ISBN 978-1-934617-29-8 (pbk.)

Printed in United States of America.
10 9 8 7 6 5 4 3 2 1

Elva Resa Publishing
8362 Tamarack Vlg Ste 119-106, St Paul, MN 55125
www.ElvaResa.com
www.MilitaryFamilyBooks.com
www.StoriesAroundTheTable.com

A portion of proceeds benefits nonprofit organizations serving military families.

Invitation

... ~ ...

THE MOST ENTERTAINING STORIES, ENGAGING
DISCUSSIONS, AND WISEST ADVICE often take place around
a table. Usually food is involved, but no matter what we eat
or drink—chicken or pizza, cheesecake or chocolate, wine or
lemonade—gathering with others opens our hearts to more
meaningful relationships and deeper conversations.

Military friends gather around the table on special occasions
and ordinary days, sometimes because we live far from our own
extended families, and sometimes simply because military friends
understand the way we live—the risks, the rewards, the nuances,
the acronyms. We don't have to explain. They know.

*Stories Around the Table: Laughter, Wisdom, and Strength in
Military Life* was inspired by those friends and gatherings. Both of
us, Karen as a Marine wife, author, and publisher at Elva Resa, and
Terri as an Air Force wife, author, and military family columnist
for *Stars and Stripes*, have over the years encountered many
military family members in need of support and friendship. We've
also met people in military life with expertise to share, some who
regularly write or talk about their experiences on social media, in
published books, at workshops, over the phone, on the radio. We
wanted to invite all of them to sit at a kitchen table together—with
us and other military families, new and seasoned—to laugh, lend

insight, and tell stories.

Alas, neither of us has a kitchen table big enough or mobile enough to make that happen for military families all over the world. So, instead, we began inviting military family members to help create a book, a collection of stories and lessons learned.

More than forty contributors accepted our invitation: wives and husbands, service members and widows, moms and dads, daughters and sisters, published authors and new writers, business leaders and founders of nonprofit organizations, volunteers and community advocates—all military family members with stories to tell. They've generously and transparently shared wisdom from their lives, gained through tragedy, trial and error, and both everyday and extraordinary circumstances.

It's our pleasure to invite you to join us, too. In this literary gathering of military friends, you'll find laughter, nourishment, clinking glasses, bare feet under the table. You might not ever meet these storytellers in person, but through their words, you may begin to know them as friends. It's our hope that their stories will encourage you, inform you, and connect you even more strongly to the wonderful life we all live.

With such a diverse group, we've dished up a varied menu, yet we haven't covered every aspect of military life. There are so many ways to live this life, so many ways to create and enjoy a military family. We've simply started a conversation, a come-as-you-are dinner party, where everyone is welcome to hear or share a story.

What are your questions? What perspective do you bring? Come, join us at this table. *Stories Around the Table* is more than a book. It's an experience, one that reaches out in multiple ways. Proceeds from this book benefit organizations that directly support military families who need help beyond what a table of friends or a book can provide. Readers can connect with authors and find ideas for hosting live *Stories Around the Table* gatherings— the best we can do to get our kitchen tables to you—by visiting **StoriesAroundTheTable.com**.

Whether you gather in a kitchen, a back yard, or the coffee shop around the corner, we wish you delicious food, sweet friendship, and a generous helping of stories to go around.

··· ~ ···

Karen Pavlicin-Fragnito
Publisher

Terri Barnes
Editor

Menu

Our Specialty: Encouraging words and sound advice from friends.

Let's Do Lunch! ~ Military Friendship

A Moveable Feast Is No Picnic ~ Transitions

Health & Soul Food ~ Mind, Body, Spirit

Bread of Sorrows ~ Grief

A Piece of (Wedding) Cake ~ Military Marriage

Eat It. It's Good for You! ~ Military Parenting

Orders to Go ~ Deployment

Check, Please ~ Careers & Finances

Coffee & Dessert ~ Sweets for the Journey

Let's Do Lunch!

Military Friendship

————————————— ... ~ ... —————————————

*"If more of us valued food and cheer and song
above hoarded gold, it would be a merrier world."*
~ J.R.R. Tolkien

Write in Pen

Diana Hartman

*I*f I could give one piece of advice to new military spouses it would be this: Ignore the standard address book advice to "Write in pencil," erasing as you move. Instead, get an address book that allows you to add pages, and write those entries in pen. Yes, it's easy enough to keep all this information on your smart phone, but if your phone is the only place you store this vital knowledge, you're always one unfortunate encounter with water or concrete from losing it all.

Record your friends' names, addresses, phone numbers, birthdays, anniversaries, and other tidbits like you mean it, because they have more meaning than you realize. Hand-carry it as you move just as you do medical records and external hard drives. I've watched friends fill moving boxes with journals, scrapbooks, recipe folders, and photo albums, while their address books stayed as thin as the day they bought them. I was the same way.

I can tell you the special ingredient in our lasagna recipe and the dates of my husband's promotions, but I struggle to remember the name of the lady who brought my daughter home after seeing her take a spill on her bike on the way home from school. I thanked the woman with a basket of muffins and a box of Band-Aids. Her house smelled of cookies and cat litter when she opened the door. But what was her name? I'd written it down—in pencil. Then we moved again, and she and I barely knew each other. So I erased it.

Among the many things our address book once contained were the names of our children's friends. When moving into one new environment after another, safety is always an issue; so is getting to know a new neighborhood and making new friends. My "address book rule" is this: My child cannot visit a friend's house until I've met the parents and have the friend's name, parents' names, address, and phone number in my book. I made time to meet the parents because I didn't want worrisome thoughts in the back of my mind about the people and environments where my kids played. The address book rule had another benefit: My address book was a more reliable tool than my children's memories when sending birthday party invitations to friends. As my children grew older and challenged the rules now and then, having their friends' information recorded and handy was like having a bullhorn, GPS, and social media all rolled into one.

While those of us who wrote in pencil stare down the thinned paper of the pages in our address books that only hold a few entries per page, pen writers have the opportunity to one day reflect on what all that information actually provides. It's not just an address book. It's the Google search engine of your own life. It's a genealogical record of your extended military family. Most of the entries in my address book are invisible now. It once documented the neighbors we've had, our children's friends, the teachers they loved (and hated), the professionals we found and relied upon, the acquaintances who moved before we had a chance to become friends, and the names of the businesses that were part of each chapter of our lives. I accepted conventional wisdom. I wrote in pencil, so I could erase them. Now I can't see them anymore.

So please don't erase. Record.

Diana Hartman is the wife of a Marine Corps veteran and a freelance writer whose work has appeared in many publications and books. Using a pencil in her address book to easily erase old entries worked for twenty-three years, until Diana realized she'd wiped out more than two decades of peripheral memory.

Dot to Dot, Friend to Friend

Stacy Allsbrook-Huisman

I was in the strange state of Ohio, and I didn't know a soul at Wright-Patterson Air Force Base. Surrounded by nothing but boxes, loads of paper, and unfinished rooms, I was already wondering how any assignment would ever compare to the one we left behind at Goodfellow AFB, Texas. My support network there was amazing. My children had best friends in the neighborhood. I had wine buddies, BFFs, and multiple shoulders to lean on. I was truly happy.

Fumbling through boxes and knick-knacks that had no home yet in my new house, I realized that I desperately needed a friend. Not just any friend, but the one friend who could give me hope for this new assignment.

Finding that friend requires "friendship dating." Every time military spouses move, we are forced to date all over again. Like the courtship process we all experienced before we got married, friendship dating is a combination of opportunity, small talk, awkward silences, probing questions, and just plain luck. It's a maddening dance, and not everyone is open to new friendships.

Life is lonely without that one friend who is ready to grab a cup of coffee at a moment's notice, the one who has an egg when I discover I'm out in mid-recipe. Hell, I just needed to find someone to list as my emergency contact at my kids' school. When I enrolled my kids, I felt like such a loser when the secretary at the new school gave me the pity face because I didn't know anyone yet.

"Don't feel sorry for me, lady," I wanted to say. "I had amazing friends at my last base."

After a move, I am often too exhausted and mentally fatigued to go in search of friends. The thought of making new friends feels like a trek up Mount Everest—insurmountable. When we arrived in Ohio, I had that sinking feeling I would never have amazing friendship connections again. But a fellow military spouse who lived several states away had already planted the seeds of my rescue.

My wonderful friend Carrie and I were stationed together in Texas a few years back, then she moved to Virginia. Carrie had a military spouse friend there named Crystal, who—like me—was moving to Ohio. Before either of us moved, Carrie had started a game of connect-the-dots with Crystal and me. She introduced us via Facebook and we became "friends" via social media.

Crystal and I traded messages, house hunting and school tips, as we each prepared to move to Ohio, she from Virginia and me from Texas. We also kept track of each other on our Facebook pages. Call it stalking, but we were watching and hoping not to see any red, glaring warning signs of crazy. Still, a social media connection is one thing. Friendship is another. So our mutual friend Carrie took a step to move our relationship to the next level.

Carrie has moved more times than I can count, including every year for the last four years—all, it seems, with grace and ease. She knows the beginnings of friendships are the toughest and most awkward. It was thoughtful of her to connect me with Crystal, even before either of us was ready to start "dating" again.

Carrie took another step to connect the dots and ensure that Crystal and I met face to face. Knowing I had a Tudor monarch obsession, Carrie gave Crystal a book about Queen Elizabeth to pass along to me. Crystal stopped by with the book a few days after I moved in, about the time I was looking around at my house full of boxes and feeling sorry for myself. It was the first time we met in person but I felt like I'd known her forever. And I loved my book.

Later that week, Crystal texted me and said she had a bottle of wine to give me. That was another thing Carrie knew about me that she had apparently passed along to Crystal: I speak wine fluently. We decided to meet in the neighborhood park.

Crystal arrived on her bike with a backpack. We sat on the park bench and she produced a beautifully adorned bottle of my favorite red wine and two plastic cups. She opened the bottle like a master and we sat together, chatting about schools and our military life while the sun began to set. It was a perfect date. We tapped our plastic glasses together and toasted Carrie, our mutual friend, who connected the dots and put us together.

When it was time to leave. I leaned over and popped the question to Crystal, "Would you mind if I listed you as my emergency contact for my children?" She responded, "Of course!" as if it had already been a foregone conclusion. And now I have that friend. I have a friend I can call anytime, someone who understands this crazy life and is more than willing to take a chance on a new face. More importantly, she carries wine in her backpack.

A life-sized reality version of the childhood game of dot-to-dot is playing out in the military spouse community as spouses connect across the globe. We are all connected and we continue playing the game by connecting others. The picture we ultimately outline is a support network like no other.

All of us have a little Carrie in us. We have friends all over. We know what they have in common. We can connect them with a few simple tools—an email, a book—the way Carrie connected me with Crystal. The more we move, the more people we know in more places, the more potential we have to connect friends with friends. Connecting those dots to create friendship is a gift. I will follow Carrie's example when the opportunity arises to help friends find each other in a new place. Friendship dating can be rough, but is easier when our fellow military spouses help us by connecting our dots.

Stacy Allsbrook-Huisman is an Air Force wife, public relations specialist, and freelance writer. Her work has appeared in *Military Spouse* magazine and GI Jobs. A hopeless extrovert, Stacy relentlessly seeks ways to connect—and connect others—in her military community.

Something's Rank

Amy Bushatz

*T*he road to military spouse prejudice hell is paved with rank insignia.

This is my confession: Without even knowing it, I have allowed prejudice to grip me. I am ashamed to admit that my choice of friends has sometimes been based on social status. Outside the gate of our military installation, those assumptions might lead me to avoid certain parts of town or certain businesses. Inside the gate, it means I subconsciously avoid certain types of people. I smile politely across the room at family readiness group functions and then go right back to talking to the people whom, I assume, are just like me.

It is a habit I have taught myself to fight.

Buying into the fear of people who are different is human nature. If I give an inch to the idea that I am superior to any other person, I have suddenly traveled a mile down the road of prejudice—and it is very difficult to come back.

Like most military brides, at first I found the rank system new and confusing. I knew what it meant to my husband. He obeyed the commands of those who outranked him and gave orders to the ones who didn't. But I knew it wasn't supposed to mean anything to me, because I am a spouse. I have no rank.

But in reality, it does mean something, even to spouses. Rank affects my social circle. Rank impacts how much money I have on payday compared to the other moms at the park. Sometimes rank dictates which housing area my family lives in.

Subconsciously, I began to rely on rank as a silent indicator of the relationship potential of spouses I met. A woman with a private first-class spouse might as well have a warning label: "Not like you—probably not friend material." I was prejudiced against people I had never met for reasons I could not confirm.

And then I met Mary Sarah.

Tattooed, pierced, and with a new hair color every time I saw her, Mary Sarah attended the same mom-and-tot playgroup on post that I did. She was proud of her rough Detroit background. She did not seem ashamed of her arrest record or that of her parents. She was clearly not part of the college graduate, NPR-listening, in-bed-by-9-o'clock crowd to whom I naturally gravitated.

My first thought was, "This is not for you."

But I stayed, I listened, and I learned. I learned that Mary Sarah isn't all Detroit-tough. She is an amazing cook, a loving mom, a caring friend, and a shoulder to lean on.

My husband was away at Ranger school when our second child was born. Mary Sarah brought me dinner. And when a few months after I met her, my father was sentenced to more than a decade in prison on a white-collar conviction—something I still have not told any of my college friends—Mary Sarah was there to cry with me.

If I had let stereotypes guide my friendships, I would never have experienced the kindness Mary Sarah had for me. And I never would have learned how much we had in common.

Stereotypes cut both ways. Launa, a retired sergeant major and the wife of an officer, has seen both sides of the rank issue. Officers' spouses, she said, may categorize enlisted members' spouses based on education and social status assumptions. But enlisted members' spouses often stereotype officers' spouses as being full of themselves just because their spouse brings home a bigger paycheck. Neither characterization is universally fair or true. Launa uses her unique position, having experience in both worlds, to encourage spouses not to judge one another by their spouses' military rank.

Because Launa's husband is a commander, she has to be careful to separate herself from his position so potential new friends aren't intimidated and don't cling to their own rank assumptions. One of the ways she does that, she says, is by not introducing herself as her husband's wife.

"Instead I just say 'I'm Launa,'" she said.

Amy, whose spouse is enlisted, is a stylish, career-driven mom with a graduate degree. New people she meets often assume, based on appearance and education, that she is an officer's spouse. But she doesn't let that stop her from forming friendships and working hard to be blind to rank and pay grade. She bases her choices and her identity on something other than her husband's career. Although I was guilty of assuming her husband was an officer when we became friends several years ago, knowing my husband's rank didn't keep her from accepting me and forming a lasting Army wife bond.

Both Amy and Launa reject the idea that military spouses are defined by a military career field. When we allow rank and prejudice to rule our military spouse lives, we shut the door to new friendships that could be the difference between finding the perfect battle buddy and languishing on our own.

For the first several years of my military spouse journey, I let rank and classism strangle my ability to build friendships with people whose lives and experiences were just what I needed. I know I'm not alone.

To the new military spouse, rank structure may seem like an easy roadmap to navigate the social challenges of military life; to the seasoned spouse, rank designation may seem like a reliable friend. But neither is true. Using rank as a way to avoid the unknown may cause you to miss out on friends and experiences that are not as far outside your comfort zone as you think.

Do yourself a favor and throw those rank ideas out the window.

Amy Bushatz is an Army wife and associate editor at Military.com, where she also serves as the managing editor of the SpouseBuzz blog. With three duty stations in her first five years of military life, Amy is ready for whatever new places and new friends Army life may bring her.

The "Ain't it Awful?" Club

Holly Scherer

In the beginning of my life as a military spouse, I was a charter member of the "Ain't It Awful?" Club. I founded new chapters with each move. Sometimes I was the only member, but usually it was pretty easy to find other complainers.

I complained constantly about things I could not do because of military life: I can't follow that career path because it would be impossible to do in this remote location. I love to garden, but I can't have a garden because there's no use in planting when we'll move before the plants mature. I can't, I can't, I can't … because, because, because.

My husband bore the brunt of my complaints, but I complained to anyone who would listen. Yes, I was that woman, the one who would stop people in the commissary checkout line to talk about how bad my life was.

I might complain about the amazing career on the East Coast I gave up to get married, or the remote location where I could not find a job in my field. I might describe the disappointing temp job I took, working on computers in a dark, musty boiler room in the basement of the local hospital. I would bemoan the ten years my husband and I struggled with infertility before having our twins, or the deployment that took him away for the first year of their lives.

Unhappiness happens when expectations do not meet reality.

Well, my expectations of married life were nothing like the reality of being married to someone in the military. I was unhappy, and I wanted everyone to know it.

One day, I learned an important life lesson from another military spouse named Kathie. Her words of wisdom came at the right time, and I took them to heart.

She said, "Focus on what you do have in your life instead of what you don't have."

This simple concept changed my life. I woke up to the fact that I was acting like a passenger in my military life rather than a participant. I was wasting my time complaining about what I didn't have in my life instead of being grateful for what I did have. I decided to stop worrying over what I didn't want in my life and start looking at what I did want and how to make it happen.

This shift in perspective—to focus on the positive, set goals, and look for possibilities—made a difference in my life at a crucial time. Our first overseas move to Bamberg, Germany, happened when war was gearing up and deployments started to become the norm. Many spouses, including me, found ourselves on our own in a foreign country, trying to figure things out while our soldiers were deployed or training to deploy.

I saw military spouses retreat into their homes and isolate themselves, afraid to venture far from the military base, intimidated by a foreign landscape and language. By then, I had two masters degrees and a lot of life experience behind me, but I still felt overwhelmed. I felt unequipped to navigate these two strange environments: the military and Germany.

My friend, Kathie, who gave me that life-changing advice, now lived in Heidelberg. She invited me to attend an orientation program there called FLAG, Families Learning About Germany. That program opened a new world to me. Instead of sitting at home petrified, I dove into life in Germany. I found military spouses to travel and explore with me. I loved the speed-limitless stretches of the Autobahn, so I was happy to drive. I partnered with other spouses who spoke the language.

After the Heidelberg program made such a difference in my life, I wanted to create a similar program at Bamberg. I joined forces with another friend, Heather, at our family service center to help create a week-long orientation program for newcomers, childcare included, called People Encouraging People Welcome Program, dubbed appropriately, PEP.

I dove in, volunteering sixty hours a week on the project. I was full of energy and excited to get up each day. My husband came home—when he was home—to hear me excitedly talk about my day. I chattered about all I was learning and the new friends I was making, instead of pouring out a litany of complaints. He also benefited from my new knowledge about resources and interesting activities in our community.

Heather and I showed military spouse newcomers how to navigate the local villages, ride public transportation, order at German restaurants, shop at German grocery stores. We told them about resources and programs available on the military installation. We saw spouses regain their independence and confidence. They met friends and realized they were not alone.

Four days into the first course, one woman shared with the group that she had asked her husband for a divorce the week before. She had decided to go back to the states with her three-year-old daughter, because she was unable to manage life in a foreign country while her husband was deployed all the time. That was before the course. A few days of making connections changed her mind. She realized she could adapt to this new life. The woman thanked me for helping to create the program and said she told her husband she no longer wanted a divorce.

I created the program to help myself and other military spouses get acclimated to Germany, but it did so much more. I developed skills for creating and directing a program, honed my speaking skills, created a network of support. On top of that, the program helped save a marriage. It was an amazing feeling. I knew I was making a difference in people's lives.

Besides engaging in life, setting big goals and proactively looking for possibilities, I learned another important practice to help me focus on the good in my life. I started keeping a gratitude journal. It's a habit I still practice. I started out by listing one hundred things I was grateful for. I add items every time I open the journal. It's a simple but powerful tool that has changed the way I look at my life. Even now, when I'm having a down day, reading through past journal entries lifts me back up.

Bad things do happen. The challenges of military life are real, but when I choose to find the good in a situation, it changes my perspective and my experience. Even when there's only a teeny tiny nugget of value, just looking for the positive keeps me from fixating on the negative.

If my early friends—those "Ain't It Awful?" Club members who heard all my complaints—could see me now, they would not believe I am the same person. They wouldn't believe how happy I am with military life or that I've coauthored four books and presented hundreds of workshops on how to discover the wonderful possibilities of this life.

My husband has embraced a sense of service to our country. As his partner on the journey, one of my responsibilities is to support him. At the same time, for my own life satisfaction and happiness, I have to focus on what is good in my life, identify what is important to me, and be open to the possibilities.

Life as a military spouse became richer and more enjoyable when I made the conscious decision to give up membership in the "Ain't It Awful?" Club and focus on gratitude instead. I cannot imagine a more meaningful life. Even the biggest complainers can change. I'm living proof.

Holly Scherer is the wife of an Army veteran, an international speaker, and coauthor of *Military Spouse Journey: Discover the Possibilities & Live Your Dreams* (Elva Resa) and *1001 Things to Love About Military Life* (Hachette). Holly loves to travel the world helping other military spouses through her workshops.

Better With Battle Buddies

Tara Crooks

*W*hen we first started out, I was the world's worst Army wife. As a new bride, I wanted nothing to do with my husband's military life. The Army was his job, not mine. The only glimpse inside the Army world I had ever had was the inside of his ROTC classroom, until the day he took me on a "field trip" to Fort Sill, Oklahoma. My first impression of the post was that it was brown. Very, very, brown. All the buildings looked the same, big, brick or—you guessed it—brown. It was all so strange. The grocery store was a "commissary." Instead of Walmart, there was a "PX." Every time I turned around, someone was asking to see my ID.

While Kevin took the Basic Officer Leader Course at Fort Sill, I stayed behind in our hometown in Missouri. As soon as we were given orders to our first assignment at Fort Hood, I was able to transfer with my job and move down to Texas on my own and wait for Kevin to join me. I found a rental house in Killeen and wondered why anyone would want to live on post. For the next eight months before Kevin joined me, I made sure I had nothing to do with the Army installation right outside my window.

When Kevin arrived, he was assigned to a unit, and shortly thereafter, the family readiness group leader called me for the first time. Here's how the conversation went:

"Hello, Tara, this is (insert name here). We're having a mandatory FRG meeting and I'll need you to bake some cookies."

My response: "Nothing is mandatory because you don't own me, and I'm not Betty Crocker."

I didn't have a clue who this FRG woman was or why she was telling me where to go and what to bake. After my hubby explained the whole FRG thing to me, I went to the meeting, and I did bring cookies. But at first, everything was foreign and intimidating. Until I met Birgit.

Birgit was the wife our unit commander, and she invited me to a battalion coffee. At that coffee, Birgit began to teach me about military life. She also introduced me to my first military spouse friend, Erin.

We were both brand new to the Army, and our husbands were in the same unit. Erin and I didn't know what we were getting into with this Army life, but we decided we'd venture it together. Having a partner made a huge difference in our ability to brave the whole new world we had been thrust into.

I had my first taste of military friendship, and it was good. Since then, I've made many more lifelong friendships.

My friend Cindy and I made the best of Fort Stewart, enduring several deployments, and had our second babies six weeks apart. Our families are still close. We've even traveled Space A to Belgium to visit them. Carla and I met at Fort Sill our second time around and immediately hit it off. We were inseparable, so much so that our friends combined our names and called us "Tarla."

Assignment by assignment, my Army friendships and

experiences grew, and so did my desire to help other military spouses connect and find support for this life I was growing to love. I met Starlett after she wrote to me and offered to write a newsletter for a fledgling project called Army Wife Talk Radio. Before long we were cohosting the podcast. Army Wife Network grew from our friendship, hard work, and mutual desire to empower other military spouses.

I now believe that the Army is not just my husband's job. It's a community and a commitment that encompasses both of us and our children.

My closest friends are my military friends. I choose them. They choose me. The common threads of this odd and challenging lifestyle pull us together, and we bond like a family. In the years since I began my Army life, my military friends have become my chosen family, a support network that makes me better and stronger.

Tara Crooks is an Army wife, cofounder of Army Wife Network, and coauthor of *1001 Things to Love About Military Life* (Hachette). She believes everyone should have a battle buddy—or a lot of them.

Stick Your Neck Out There

Lori Hensic

*O*ne year into my relationship with a United States Marine, I had little or no knowledge of the military community and no military spouse friends. My relationship with my wife, Shaina, began after graduate school. By then, I already had an established group of close friends from school and work, and I never imagined I would need a different kind of friend to provide support for the challenges military life would pose. But soon it became clear that there were some things my civilian friends didn't understand. They were too far removed from my experiences and struggles in military life to provide the support I needed.

Shaina was stationed at Camp Pendleton in San Diego, California. I lived in San Francisco, near most of my closest friends and my family. I had an awesome job and an amazing apartment in the heart of the city, but I didn't have my wife. And no amount of chipper Southwest flight attendants singing funny songs before takeoff lightened the load of the constant weekend travel demanded by our long distance relationship. So I found a new job, gave my landlord notice, exchanged tearful hugs with friends and family, and moved to Southern California.

Within a month of moving, the reality of military life hit me. Shaina was swept away by temporary duty assignments at a rate that made my head spin. While all of this seemed normal to her, I was lost and confused. The travel the Marine Corps required of her affected me more than it had during our long-distance relationship. I quickly discovered that military life would now impact me much more directly. I questioned whether moving was the right decision. When I reached out to others back home, I got comments like, "At least you're together now." The time apart from Shaina was different now in a way that my civilian friends—while supportive—couldn't understand. I felt alone and vulnerable.

It was daunting to think of reaching out for new friends in a new home and a new environment, but when a weekend military spouse event came to our installation, I took a chance and signed up. I made Shaina go with me. I was far too nervous to go alone. We sat at an empty table in the back. There were at least twenty other tables full of young military spouses, all chatting with each other as if they were lifelong friends—which was even more intimidating. Attendees were divided up into break-out groups based on how many kids they had. We don't have kids, so we were soon surrounded by women who were several years younger than us, many under twenty-one. I felt old. Disconnected. How could these young women be the support system I was looking for when the age difference alone implied we had very little in common?

I was terrified what their reaction would be when they found out that the woman sitting next to me was not my friend but the love of my life. As the conversation progressed, the natural pleasantries and standard questions that pop up with introductions were asked, and it didn't take long before the group realized Shaina and I were a couple.

And the sky didn't fall.

The women were receptive, interested in our story, and immediately rattled off resources that would help me get better acquainted with military life. Because the group was so young, they were almost as new to military life as I was. They could relate to my confusion about my new life. What first appeared to be a group of young, unseasoned military spouses turned out to be a table full of welcoming, vibrant young women with whom I had more in common than I expected. Some at the table were not as supportive. Some were silent. But those who were friendly far outshined those who weren't. I exhaled a sigh of relief that had been waiting years to come out.

The event gave me hope. I had allowed my fear of acceptance get the better of me and limit my chances of making new friends. Isolation was my biggest enemy, causing me to miss out on connecting with other military family members. I discovered that sticking my neck out wasn't as dangerous as I thought. This event alone would not forge close friendships; I would still have to figure that out on my own, but it was an encouraging start.

Civilian life usually creates groups of like-minded people, joined by mutual interests, a set of shared experiences, or even simply geographic location. The military community is made up of people from a variety of places and backgrounds. We have military life in common, but making friends can be complicated by our different experiences.

Diversity contributes to the beauty of the military community. The richness of that diversity—of gender, race, ethnicity, religion,

sexual orientation, political affiliation, backgrounds, and beliefs—
is a shining reflection of our nation. No matter where we are
assigned, we will encounter folks from all over the world. With
such tremendous diversity, it can be challenging at times to find
common ground. But we will always have the demands of military
life in common, demands no one should try to survive alone.

I found I was least successful at making friends when I tried
to be who I thought the military wanted me to be. I was more
successful when I was true to myself. In the process of making
friends in the military community, I learned not to let others'
thoughts or beliefs discourage me from continuing to put myself
out there, and more importantly, to remind myself to make sure my
thoughts or beliefs are not doing that to anyone else.

Sticking my neck out and looking for friends turned out to be
less frightening—and far more rewarding—than isolating myself in
military life.

Lori Hensic is a Marine wife, the director of research and policy at The
American Military Partners Association, a university professor, and the head
of medication safety for two community hospitals. Her favorite job is being a
mother to her furry, four-legged child, Toby.

A Moveable Feast Is No Picnic

Transitions

——————————— ··· ~ ··· ———————————

*"If you are lucky enough to have lived in Paris
as a young man, then wherever you go
for the rest of your life, it stays with you,
for Paris is a moveable feast."*
~ Ernest Hemingway

First, You're Gonna Hate It

Terri Barnes

"You're gonna love it," enthused my friend Janice when she heard we had orders to Germany. "But first, you're gonna hate it."

She was wrong, of course, but I didn't contradict her out loud. I thought it was good insight for my children, then nine, twelve, and fifteen, who were listening in. They were understandably hesitant about changing schools and leaving friends. To them, moving to Europe meant leaving behind the familiar once again. It was good for them to hear that it was okay to hate it before they learned to love it.

But she was dead wrong about me. I was never going to hate it. I would love this assignment from day one. After a lifetime of being in a military family, going to Europe was the dream I thought might never come true. Then the miracle happened. We got orders to Ramstein Air Base. I could hardly wait.

We had been overseas twice before in the Pacific theater, so I knew about difficult adjustments. Moving to Europe wouldn't be like that.

Janice said, "Give yourself at least three months to adjust," and she listed the little frustrations that could add up to a big case of culture shock. I smiled and nodded, knowing none of them would faze me.

I had already lived outside the continental United States multiple times in my military lifetime. One of those assignments was Japan, where I learned to drive on the other side of the road and eat raw fish.

Europe? Bring it on.

My friend's words came back to me a few weeks later. I was pounding on the steering wheel of my German rental car—diesel and standard shift, the only car available—which I had stalled for the third time while trying to enter a traffic roundabout. I finally got into the roundabout, only to discover it was not the one that would take me to the post office. All the roundabouts looked the same. I was lost. The car stalled again.

"Why does everything have to be so hard?" I shouted to no one in particular. "I just want to check my mail!" My children stared at their mother, who had apparently lost her mind.

I was still finding my way around base and had not even ventured outside the front gate. I had not yet seen the Europe of my dreams. Far from it.

We had arrived at Ramstein in the middle of a July heat wave and found out quickly that air conditioning was the exception, not the rule. The BX was stifling; so was the community center. Every time we walked into our room at billeting we were wilted by the wave of hot air that met us at the door. It was even hotter inside than out, because all our windows opened toward the steaming asphalt of the parking lot. The lot absorbed the heat all day and gave it back at night.

Our places of refuge were the commissary and the library,

where sane minds and air conditioning prevailed. But we could only hang out in frozen foods or nonfiction for so long. The rest of the time we felt like we were baking in a holding pattern, waiting for our house to be ready, waiting for our car to arrive, waiting for our utilities to be connected, waiting for this dream assignment to start feeling less like a nightmare.

"First, you're gonna hate it," Janice had said. So this is what she was talking about.

My second assignment as a young military wife had been to Andersen Air Force Base, Guam. A US territory thousands of miles from the mainland, Guam has a distinct island culture. I didn't know what culture shock was at the time, but I acquired a bad case of it there. I thought my job as a military spouse was to be happy no matter what, no matter where. So I didn't tell anyone—not even my husband—about my struggle to adjust. I thought there must be something wrong with me. Who could be miserable on a tropical island? I could. It wasn't all bad, by any means, but isolating myself made it a difficult assignment.

A few years later, when we got orders to Japan, I knew I couldn't live like that again. I told my husband he needed to know up front that I might not like living there, that it might take me time to settle in. He was supportive and willing to hear my frustrations, and I promised myself and him that I wouldn't go around complaining to everyone else. Because I had a release valve and reasonable expectations, adjusting to Japan was surprisingly easy. I acknowledged the culture shock and the adjustments and gave myself permission not to love everything about it.

Germany was a different story, or so I thought. Living and traveling in Europe had always been my dream. After adjusting to and enjoying my time in Japan, I couldn't imagine I would have any trouble adjusting to a Western culture. How different could it be? Enough to make me crazy, it turns out.

When I dreamed about living in Europe, I was focused on the "Europe" part, not the "living" part. No matter where we live, there are bills to pay and laundry to do. An assignment in Europe is not a three-year vacation. It's life in a foreign country, where I had to do all the things I normally had to do, but not quite the way I was used to doing them. After twenty-plus years and two other overseas assignments, I still experienced culture shock.

The German village where we lived is picturesque, but it's a real place, not a postcard. They speak a different language there, and they have different ideas about methods for paying bills and how long it should take to get the Internet working at my house, among other things.

Janice was right on both counts. I hated Germany for a few weeks, and then I loved it, not because it was suddenly picture perfect, but because I adjusted my image of what living in Germany should and would be like. We finally moved into our house, got a phone, and figured out how to sort the recyclables, which is harder than it sounds.

I let go of my unrealistic expectations and some of my American bias about the way things should be done. I learned to love Germany, not in spite of the differences but because of them.

Now when I talk to someone who is moving to Germany, or

Japan or Guam, or anywhere, I give them the same advice that gave me hope and reminded me to set reasonable expectations.

"You're gonna love it," I tell them. "But first, you're gonna hate it."

Terri Barnes is the military family columnist for *Stars and Stripes* and the author of *Spouse Calls: Messages From a Military Life* (Elva Resa). In her life as an Air Force wife, Terri has hated—and then grown to love—four overseas assignments.

Challenging My Normal

Starlett Henderson

I was tired of sighing and wondering. I wanted something to happen. College life was not as exciting, not even as challenging as I had hoped. So one day, I stopped by the military recruiting office and joined the Army.

It was unlike me to sign on the dotted line without days or weeks of contemplating the change or effects of that change—without consulting anyone—but that's what I did. When I joined the Army, courage came first. Reflection, planning, and aligning the horse with the cart came later. It was completely outside my normal, but it was right.

In hindsight, my gut had done all the thinking for me, so when people ask me, "Should I follow my head or my heart?" my answer is: "Follow your gut."

Joining the Army was not a "Paper or plastic?" "Skim milk or whole?" decision. It was a big step outside my normal, but I did it. I joined the Army, and in that situation, challenging my normal without deliberation worked for me.

It turned out to be a good decision—even if accidental—and because of that I've found it easier to be courageous at other crossroads in my life, including knowing when it was time to leave the Army.

After that, I both applied to and decided against law school, left a government job even though my boss and coworkers said I was crazy, had a second child before I adjusted to having the first one, and so on. Each of these was a situation where it would have been normal or easier for me to go right, but I chose left.

Doing the opposite of the expected turned into a habit in my life. This was especially true when I became a work-at-home, public person as the cofounder of Army Wife Network. I am usually a behind-the-scenes kind of person. I like to work alone. Growing up, I dreamed frequently of a commute, promotions, structure, a desk job, and a nine-to-five life. I thought it would come easy.

Instead, I grabbed a job that was hard. I had to stretch outside my comfort zone. I had to stand up and speak to large groups of military spouses. I had to learn to balance home and office. I had to learn to work with a partner, one of the most gregarious personalities in the military spouse community.

Truthfully, if my work at AWN had not been in support of military families, I would have quickly given it up in favor of something more suited to my personality. Through faith and the support of family—both genetic and military—I was encouraged to challenge my normal once again.

My experience with AWN ranks right up there with joining the Army as something that changed my life for the better. My previous normal is not good enough anymore. I will always measure my next adventure by whether I will grow as much and give as much as I did at AWN.

My gut also dictated when it was time to challenge my normal again and leave AWN. I left without knowing my next adventure, taking comfort in the fact that I didn't get this far with meticulous planning. Following my gut and challenging my normal catapulted me farther than I ever dared dream or plan.

Some people make changes easily, challenging their normal at every opportunity. Some accept difficult circumstances more gracefully than others. Then there's the rest of us, including me. I like the comfortable, but my past experiences remind me to mix it up a little. I don't want to settle for normal, when challenging my normal is so much more rewarding.

Starlett Henderson is an Army veteran, Army wife, cofounder of Army Wife Network, and coauthor of *1001 Things to Love About Military Life* (Hachette). Challenging the normal is a strategy Starlett recommends—and has seen work—time and time again.

The Perfect Move

Brenda Pace

When women start sharing stories about childbirth, each story has a kind of one-upmanship as the speaker delivers her blow-by-blow march into motherhood. Talking to military spouses about moving and transition can have the same level of intensity and competition as dueling delivery room narratives.

Everyone in the military has heard a few PCS horror stories. My husband and I know one military family whose household goods sunk to the bottom of the Pacific Ocean on an ill-fated cargo ship and another who lost track of their worldly possessions somewhere between Israel and the United States.

Sometimes even a simple door-to-door stateside move can go wrong. My husband planned the perfect move from Fort Leavenworth, Kansas, to Fort Bragg, North Carolina. It should have been easy. Our shipment would not have to be in storage but would go directly from one house to the other. We would simply synchronize watches with the truck driver when he left our old house and meet him at the door of our new one.

On the day of the perfect move, everything went fine until it was time for delivery. My husband showed up at our new house at the right time, but the truck driver and all our household goods did not. My husband waited a day, another day, and yet, another day.

He called the moving company and was informed the truck had experienced mechanical problems. The dispatcher assured him our belongings were on their way. After three more days, the moving company finally admitted they had not heard from the truck driver since he left our first house. However, they had received a call from someone in Virginia who reported that a truck matching the description of our truck, carrying all our possessions, was abandoned on the side of the road.

Eventually, we were reunited with our property and, surprisingly, there was nothing missing and very little damage. From this experience and others, I've learned a few lessons about transition.

First, no matter how much planning I do, some things are out of my control. I do not have control over an alcohol-impaired and irresponsible truck driver who abandons my household goods on the side of the road in the wrong state.

I do have control over what I do and say. No amount of pacing, worrying, fussing, complaining, or crying could deliver our things to our door. I may have done some of that—okay, I did a lot of that—but I got a grip and functioned anyway.

Second, while it was frustrating to wait and worry over the condition of our stuff, I realized it was only stuff. Stuff can be replaced. In subsequent moves, I hand-carried anything I felt I could not live without. For me, those essentials were not furnishings or clothing, but objects with sentimental value, such as photos and memorabilia.

Third, waiting for life to be perfect is a habit I do not want to cultivate. As we waited for our shipment to arrive in North Carolina, we felt completely unsettled. I confess I sometimes have waited through an entire assignment like that—waiting for everything to be aligned so that I could be content. As I waited for things to be like they were at Fort Fill-in-the-Blank, I wasted time and energy being disappointed. I waited for friends like I had at my last duty station, leadership that set an ideal command tone, a training schedule that was more conducive to family life, an assignment that was on our dream sheet, ad infinitum. While I was waiting for perfection, I missed opportunities right in front of me.

The fourth and most important lesson I learned is that I make the choice to be content. During one particularly difficult transition, I read a quote that is forever branded in my mind: "Two women looked out through prison bars; one saw mud, the other stars." Too often, I have allowed complaint and comparison to rob me of the joy of the moment. It's taken me too long, but I finally realize that I choose the lens through which I view my circumstances. I don't have to love a place or a situation for it to be worthwhile.

Some duty stations have provided me with more training ground for cultivating contentment than others, but there have always been valuable lessons to learn, and treasured relationships to enjoy wherever Uncle Sam has sent our family.

This is a time-honored truth for military spouses. Historical records describe Martha Washington journeying to the encampments of the Revolutionary War during the long winter months. Mrs. Washington was born into the social elite and could have stayed comfortably at home, yet she made this grueling trip each winter to tend wounded soldiers, host guests, encourage other military wives, and support her soldier husband. She wrote: "The greater part of our happiness or misery depends upon our dispositions, and not upon our circumstances."

Everyone has moving stories, some good and some bad. Very few are perfect. Uncle Sam writes the narrative of where and when for those stories, but he doesn't control our contentment. That part of the story is ours to determine.

Brenda Pace is the wife of an Army veteran, a popular speaker, and an author. Her books include *Medals Above My Heart: The Rewards of Being a Military Wife* (Broadman and Holman). Now that her husband is retired from the military, Brenda actually misses the words, "I got orders!"

Drawn and Quartered

Janine Boldrin

*S*ome people greet their new neighbors with a friendly wave or even a meal on the day they move in. I met my neighbors when they were screaming at each other from their respective front steps. The argument, something to do with mowing the lawn, ended with a crescendo of shouting and hand gestures that left me wondering what alternate universe I had stumbled into when I moved into military family quarters on an Army post.

Some people absolutely love living on post while others consider it a form of torture. Hearing stories, like the one about my screaming neighbors, can frighten people away from even considering military housing.

My Army family has lived on post for different reasons at different assignments. Sometimes the choice was based on my husband's job or the availability of rentals in the community. Sometimes the length of stay for an assignment influenced our decision. The social side of post living is also a big factor for us. It's a place our children can feel understood, surrounded by children who live the same life they do. There is an ease to moving into a military neighborhood, a community with so much in common.

Every military family has many things to consider when choosing where to live: cost, availability, commute, school districts, and more. Military housing may be the best choice at one assignment, but not at the next.

Living on post can provide an instant community. Six months into my husband's third deployment, I felt like I was losing my mind. I couldn't keep the kids from fighting or the car from breaking down. The snow wouldn't stop falling. My neighbors on post got me through it. As housing maintenance crews struggled to clean driveways, my neighbors showed up to help shovel the snow and ice in front of my house. Nothing warms the heart of a spouse with a deployed soldier on a snowy day more than the arrival of someone with a shovel and a smile.

When the kids got sick, an on-post friend offered to pick up food at the commissary. The military hospital was only a few blocks away, which came in handy way too many times during that deployment. When I cut my hand on a can of peaches and had to get a tetanus shot—yes, everything happened during that deployment—I knew I could still find a way to get my son to his basketball practice. His coach lived down the street. Long nights alone were less frightening to me knowing other military families were only a few feet away if anything happened.

Anyone who has lived in military housing knows it isn't Shangri-La. Take my porch-screaming neighbors, please. There were times when I wondered how I could live near them for two years, which turned into three. The trouble evolved from that first day of yelling to barking dogs to the television blaring through our shared walls until 3:00 a.m.

My wonderful backyard neighbor made up for the next-door

crazies. With her, I could laugh and talk while the kids played. My neighbor across the street was a good running partner. My oldest son's best friend lived two blocks away, and my younger son's favorite playmate lived up the hill. Post living meant our kids could run through the woods and walk to school in a safe environment. It was a place where we appreciated knowing everyone in the blocks surrounding our home.

Lots of good comes with accepting a government-issued house key. But, no, it isn't perfect.

I cringe when I remember the faux-wood-linoleum flooring that I could never get clean, but then I loved that I could call maintenance—without opening my checkbook—when my dishwasher misbehaved. The garage wasn't quite big enough, but most military housing comes with a dog-friendly backyard fence. And of course, there's the ten-minute commute for my active duty husband.

Yes, there are those situations that drive us all nuts. The kid who won't stop asking to play on your trampoline. Whoops, I think that was my kid! The car that is always parked at the end of your driveway. Yes, I did hit it once. The leaky faucet that maintenance never manages to actually fix, in spite of repeated promises. My husband finally figured it out.

When I think about it, I've had similar annoyances living off post. Once, we unknowingly bought a house only a few blocks away from a meth lab. That was during my husband's second deployment. No, I didn't feel safe being awakened at 2:00 a.m. by a police raid at the house down the street. I feel safer with my military neighbors, even the screaming ones and their barking dogs.

On post, I remember the snowy day when I saw young soldiers, who had been out on a run, taking a detour to sled down our hill with my kids. I've had the chance to meet friends with whom I had nothing in common the day I moved in but everything in common the day I moved out. There were recipes handed over backyard fences, baby monitors exchanged before doing the school pickup, block parties, and late night book club.

These are the reasons people choose to live on post.

Years ago, an older couple from my hometown church were excited to hear I was engaged to a soldier. They had lived a military life themselves, moving from post to post, in the United States and overseas. They said living on different installations and the friends they made along the way was the best part of their lives; it was a life like no other, with memories and people they'd never forget.

"We loved living on post," said the wife.

"You're lucky," said her husband.

I'm sure we will look back and remember those times on post as some of our favorite memories of military life. In fact, I know we will. Even if some of those memories are a little crazy.

Janine Boldrin is an Army wife and writer whose work has appeared in *The Huffington Post*, *Military Spouse*, and *Good Housekeeping*. Janine doesn't always live on post, but when she does, she thinks the benefits outweigh all the crazy.

Why I'm Off Base

Chris Pape

My wife has been in the Air Force for twenty years, yet she has rarely lived on a military installation. When we first met, she was stationed at F.E. Warren Air Force Base in Cheyenne, Wyoming, but lived in Fort Collins, Colorado, nearly an hour and a whole state away. I had no idea she was active duty Air Force until after our second date. From the beginning, we've shared a desire to separate work life from family life, and that's one reason we've never lived on an Air Force base.

This philosophy usually leads to the following question: "Don't you want to live closer to all the family benefits a base provides?" The cocktail party answer is that we're both very proud of Dana's career, but we don't want that to define who we are.

Since I'm among friends who have experience with this crazy military lifestyle, let me elaborate. I am well aware that many military families absolutely love on-base living and couldn't imagine driving thirty minutes to the commissary, the exchange, or work. Living away from base isn't for everyone. But similar geographic benefits are also available for those who choose to live elsewhere, away from base or post. No matter our location over the last twelve years, we have always been close to great schools, hospitals, shopping, dining, and activities. In fact, everywhere we've lived has been close enough to a military installation to enjoy all the military benefits and still maintain contact with the civilian world.

Frankly, one important reason we've stayed off base is purely pragmatic. We have been disappointed by the quality of living conditions offered by military housing, including the age of the facilities and their proximity to other families. We like a little space.

A sense of ownership is also important to us. We have lived in our share of dumps, but at least they were our dumps. We owned them, so we could paint the walls whatever colors we wanted and renovate however we saw fit. We didn't need anyone's permission to do so. Also, we feel it's important for military families to participate in our local communities. For us, there's no better way to do this than to live off base.

Since getting married, Dana and I have owned three homes and rented two. Many people, including our financial advisor, ask why we choose to buy instead of simply rent. In other words, why do we potentially put ourselves at financial risk every few years simply to own a house? The biggest reason is probably for the sake of my sanity. We both know that the Air Force already controls nearly every decision we make, from the color and style of Dana's hair to when and where we move. My wife is also aware of the many sacrifices I've made for the sake of her career. She knows that surrendering even more control over my life makes me depressed and angry. Kind of like the Incredible Hulk, but without the muscles. As a male military spouse who battles emasculation issues, I feel good when I have a role in deciding where and how we live. Our happy and healthy marriage is worth the financial risk of selling our home every few years.

Besides my sanity and our happy marriage, I've found several other advantages to having our own property. Privacy for one. Whether it was playing in the cornfields of central Ohio as a child, or getting lost in a crowd when I was in college, I've always needed an escape. I imagine base housing doesn't offer much respite from military life. The people who live on base work with their neighbors and relax with their coworkers. My wife works for the military, and I am a military spouse, but that doesn't define who we are. We have many different interests, hobbies, and future plans that don't include the Air Force. Having a home that is a retreat away from military life is essential for us.

Additionally, life off base makes it a little easier for our careers to coexist. When looking for work after each PCS, I believe having a civilian address at the top of my resume looks more permanent than one from the local Air Force base. Living within the community makes me more relatable in a job interview. In today's tough job market, every advantage helps. Living away from base also allows us to be more centrally located, convenient to both our jobs. While in Little Rock, Arkansas, we lived between our workplaces. I worked twenty-five minutes west of our home, while Dana's office at Little Rock AFB was twenty-five minutes east.

Owning a home has helped us work as a team. One of our hobbies is renovating and remodeling our houses. We've found no healthier way to share our time than working together on our house and yard. Not only does laying five yards of mulch, remodeling our kitchen, and chopping down a tree make me feel more like a man, but it's also a great way for the two of us to share our time. When the weather is bad, we're usually sprucing up the inside of our house. We spend these hours talking and growing closer while we're working together.

During our last PCS, we decided to rent instead of own, and we ended up spending most of our weekends watching sports at a bar. We tried to find other hobbies, but nothing really stuck. Don't get me wrong, we love our beer and games, but this isn't the healthiest of lifestyles when it's our only release. So we've decided that home ownership is the best lifestyle for us.

Home ownership in the military isn't without its difficulties, and it isn't for everybody. It takes guts, dedication, and creativity to make it work, especially when you know you'll have to sell in a few years. Choosing the right house requires experience and luck, but the basic question we ask ourselves before buying any house is, "Can we sell it?" To answer this, we need to know if the house is priced right, including homeowner association fees and taxes, located in a popular neighborhood with a good school district, and built with a popular floor plan by a solid builder. The house we prefer usually takes second place to the one we know we can sell. We've learned these lessons the hard way, and over the last ten years we've probably lost more money in real estate than the average civilian homeowner. Our losses have taught us to pay attention to several different variables, including the length of our anticipated time in the area, the economic conditions, and major employers in our region. Each of these criteria can affect the resale value of a home and the potential for profit or loss.

Every military family is different and needs to learn what works for them. This is a crazy, stressful life we lead, and finding a comfortable place to call home is one of the most important decisions we can make for the health and happiness of our families. This is what keeps me off base and on track.

Chris Pape is an Air Force husband, professional videographer, and the founder of a video-based website for male military spouses, MachoSpouse.com. He was named Air Force Military Spouse of the Year in 2014. It took him ten years to realize he was a military spouse, but now Chris makes the most of every day.

Seven Things on the Table

Starlett Henderson

*a*t our house, when I yell "Dinner time!" everyone knows it is time to put seven things on the table: silverware, serving ware, cups, plates, food, drinks, and condiments.

Seems like an easy thing, but before we mapped it out, we had a lot of getting up and down in the middle of a meal for things we forgot. "Where's the salt?" and "I need a spoon!" We all knew what should be on the table, but we didn't have a checklist to define the routine and make sure everything we needed was available.

Routines are helpful in a variety of situations. They help overcome anxiety by making your choices and actions more predictable. They are especially helpful when moving to a new place. Having a routine and a checklist to follow is like bringing the comfort of home along with you.

Do you know which services your family needs to feel settled in and happy in a new town? Maybe your top ten list includes a source of organic or farm fresh vegetables, a math tutor, or a pet groomer. Does your family have a list and does everyone know from the beginning what you are seeking? The more family members who are clued in and looking for items on your list, the easier the hunt for your necessities and new local favorites.

Our family's list includes a church, library, grocery store, hairdresser, post office, some sort of refuge—like a gym, spa, or park— a doctor, and a veterinarian. Before we developed our checklist, we would get to a new town and be all over the map. We'd know we were missing something, and then have to scramble when someone had a toothache, or I needed to mail a package, or when we simply wanted movies for family night. Now that we have our checklist, we locate the essentials right away. We know what we need and where to find it.

Each new place or situation calls for a routine, and old routines call for an update. Even now, I realize I need to modify my table preparation checklist to eight things on the table. I need to add napkins to my list, and while I'm at it, I'll make sure the supply isn't running low.

Starlett Henderson is an Army veteran, Army wife, cofounder of Army Wife Network, and coauthor of *1001 Things to Love About Military Life* (Hachette). She says having a routine is the secret to getting settled in a new place and getting help setting the table for dinner.

Health & Soul Food

Mind, Body, Spirit

———————————— ··· ~ ··· ————————————

"A spoonful of sugar helps the medicine go down."
~ Mary Poppins

Alive Day

Kristin Henderson

My husband, Frank, and I were having a bad day. We were on the Beltway around Washington, DC, headed for Walter Reed National Military Medical Center. We were fighting about something stupid, I don't even remember what anymore. Oh wait, yes I do. I thought he was driving like a maniac and he thought I was a controlling bitch.

At Walter Reed, we were supposed to meet up with my coworker but I wasn't sure where. We got out in a parking garage and slammed our doors. Frank went one way and I went another. Eventually, we did all wind up in the same place: outside the locked psychiatric ward, waiting for the staff to let us in. We were pushing a cart piled high with pizzas and sodas. It was the Fourth of July and we were the party.

I work for a nonprofit that provides practical support to injured service members and their families. I'm the communications director. But on that day, along with Frank, I was simply a volunteer. My coworker's job is to organize social events and outings, and normally when she needs help she puts out the word to our 1,300 volunteers.

The psych ward is different. The rules are stricter than in the regular patient wards, the stakes of a misstep higher. She knew me, knew my husband is a Navy chaplain, and figured she could count on us to be steady, low key, positive. So naturally, we showed up ready to scratch each other's eyeballs out.

We faked it. We set out the pizzas, poured sodas, made casual conversation with the few who were chatty, gave the others their space. Frank and I have both done this sort of thing before, especially Frank. As a chaplain, he's visited patients in psychiatric facilities. But after a while it finally hit me—this was the first time either one of us had done it since his last Afghanistan tour.

He served in the combat hospital at Kandahar Air Field. He spent time in the bloody trauma bays with NATO doctors, nurses, and corpsmen, in the morgue with the soldiers who prepared the American dead to go home. His collateral duties included taking pictures in the operating room for training and documentation: amputations, brain surgeries, exposed beating hearts. He sat at the bedside of dying Afghan soldiers and children. He became the resident expert in how to prepare a Muslim body for burial. He listened to anyone who needed someone to talk to. Then he came home to another pressure cooker assignment. His head was not in a good place. Two years later, he'd barely gotten his equilibrium back. There'd been a lot of bad days for both of us in those two years.

In the car after leaving the psych ward, I asked, "So on the way over here, were you thinking about your own combat stress?"

"Yeah," he said, like, duh.

"That didn't even occur to me. I'm sorry."

"Me, too."

A few miles later I said, "I'm really glad we did that."

"Yeah," he said. "Me, too."

***

That's the thing about helping. You often feel like you get more out of it than the people you help. It gives life meaning to be part of something larger than yourself. It's an honor to be in a position, even on the bad days, to be able to make a small difference for others. It's why I love being a military spouse. It's why I love my job.

It's not that my job isn't heartbreaking sometimes. There are many bad days for the families who rush to the bedsides of loved ones wounded by war. Frank's done three combat tours, one in Iraq, two in Afghanistan. I know that could have been us. Some days you just have to cry for all the painful, body-altering, mind-twisting, life-changing injuries, as well as the relationships and marriages that crumble under the stress.

This job can also be frustrating. One of the things that frustrates me most is the injustice faced by family caregivers. They're usually spouses, sometimes parents, girlfriends, or boyfriends. When their military loved one is injured, they're essentially drafted into the service of our country. They drop everything, leave their homes and jobs and sometimes children, and go stay at a faraway military hospital to help with the recovery. They may be there a few months or a few years, sacrificing for their wounded warrior and their country. And for that, they're often fired.

One caregiver was told to choose between her injured daughter and her job. She chose her daughter and was fired by email. Another caregiver's boss came to Walter Reed National Military Medical Center and fired her right there in the lobby. Meanwhile, her son was in ICU fighting for his life after losing both legs. It's especially tough for the parents of the injured. When people that age leave their jobs to care for a relative, they lose on average $325,000 in lifetime income, including lost wages, Social Security, and pensions. And that's not right.

I wish jobs like mine weren't necessary, but as long as there are wars, I know they will be necessary. Despite all the frustration and heartbreak, my job is awe-inspiring. Or maybe it's the frustrating, heartbreaking parts that make it so inspiring.

For the family caregivers of injured service members, every waking minute is filled with helping their injured loved one get ready for the day, then get through seven hours of appointments for wound care, traumatic brain injury, and post-traumatic stress support, physical and occupational therapy, dermatology, prosthetics, and adaptive sports training. After that there are more hours of rehab on their own, medications to manage, and paperwork to fill out, meals to prepare, laundry to do, and in many cases, children to care for.

The caregivers who stick it out are one tough, dedicated, joke-cracking bunch, and the relationships that survive deserve a standing ovation. Along the way, there's the empowering joy of celebrating the triumphs of recovery from devastating injuries: From the first halting steps on new prosthetics to the first lap around the track on running blades; from overcoming fears of crowds to going back to school to start a new life.

Doing my small part to help determined, courageous, resilient people like that is a privilege. It's a privilege that's open to anyone. More than 50,000 service members have been injured in Iraq and

Afghanistan, and eventually they all leave the hospital and go home. But most of their hometowns aren't ready for them. Only a small percentage of Americans today know what it's like to send loved ones to war and welcome them home, much less welcome them home with a serious physical or psychological injury.

As a result, community safety nets have giant gaps that combat-injured families can fall through when they leave the hospital. The government can't do everything. It's going to take volunteers, military and civilian, neighbors helping neighbors, to ensure this generation of combat-injured families gets the support they deserve.

***

So now I've just seen Frank off on another deployment. Once again I've handed over this precious, irreplaceable human being I love to a purpose larger than both of us. I'm at work, missing him, having kind of a bad day. I'm sorting through photos that have been given to us by injured service members and their families. We'll use them to raise funds and awareness.

As I look at the photos I'm sorting—at the scars and missing limbs and incredibly young faces—I think about the people who ask me, "Isn't your job depressing?" I imagine them looking over my shoulder at these photos, because if they did, they'd see the answer to that question. Most of the people in them are smiling.

I can't help smiling myself. I've come to understand that even though there are bad days, even though recovering from a devastating injury is harder than most people know, these people are smiling because the unique, irreplaceable human beings they love are alive. Combat-injured families have a whole new holiday to celebrate. They call it Alive Day, the anniversary of the day the enemy tried to kill their loved one—and failed.

And that's a damn good day.

Kristin Henderson is a Navy wife, communications director for the Yellow Ribbon Fund, and author of several books, including *While They're At War* (Houghton Mifflin Harcourt). On good days, Kristin advocates for military families in her adopted hometown of Washington, DC. She does it on bad days, too, but those days require more wine and chocolate.

Taking My Medicine

Sarah Smiley

*A*stronaut Buzz Aldrin. Former Pittsburgh Steelers quarterback Terry Bradshaw. Actor Marlon Brando. Comedian Jim Carrey. Princess Diana. Charles Dickens. Tolstoy. Billy Joel. And President Abraham Lincoln.

Especially President Lincoln.

These notable people have all battled depression. For most of my life, I counted myself as one of them—not for being notable, but for suffering from depression. After a serious case of postpartum depression when my first son was born thirteen years ago, made more difficult by my husband's looming first deployment, I started taking medication for it.

Over the last decade, however, I was doing extremely well. I decided maybe I no longer identified with the likes of the list above, and it was time to stop taking my medicine. I mean, I'm not having any more babies, so postpartum depression is no longer a concern. And I hadn't had a major episode in thirteen years.

So, against the advice of my doctor, and despite my husband jokingly telling me he would pay me to keep taking the medicine, I started tapering my dose.

For a while, I did great. Then, after about six months, in the middle of winter, everything went out of control. I couldn't find a reason to get up in the morning. Even things that used to make me smile—finishing a knit hat, going to my kids' school functions, eating dinner as a family—brought nothing. I felt hollowed out and flat. Worse, I couldn't stop crying, and I didn't know why.

I explain the feelings of depression to my husband, who has never experienced a true depression, like this: It's a creeping feeling, a heaviness that is there when you first open your eyes in the morning. Shopping for Christmas presents is an effort, holiday music an annoyance. Deadlines, bills, cleaning—even cutting my own toenails—seem like enormous obstacles. But mostly, I feel like a shell of a person.

It doesn't matter what triggers the depression. The triggers are different for everyone. But anyone who has been through it knows that the abyss quickly feels like it will swallow you whole.

That winter, in a moment of desperation, because, of course, my husband was away on duty, I reached out to a counselor. My boys had started to recognize that something was wrong, and with my husband gone so often, I am their constant. I could see the worry in their eyes.

I knew things were bad, but I held out hope that I could be one of those "regular" people who don't need antidepressants, people who can go for a jog and feel better. What finally changed my mind was when I was crying in my room and my youngest son slipped a note under the door. "It's worse when you are sad," he wrote.

But getting help isn't always easy. In fact, getting help is one of the hardest, most important things anyone will ever do. There were other people in the waiting room when I arrived for my first appointment. We were all from different socioeconomic starting-points, but we were at the same finish line, with weary bodies, tear-stained faces and wearing yesterday's sweatpants.

When a woman from the insurance department came to talk to me, I noticed she was wearing a Talbots dress. I had seen it at Talbots two months earlier, back when I did things like get dressed. Two months ago, I might have mentioned the dress to the woman. But not that day. We didn't have the same rapport we might have had another time. I had slipped into a different category. It was "us" and "them." I was "us." She was "them."

I began taking my medicine again. Any time I felt smaller for doing so, I asked myself, "Would a diabetic withhold medicine from herself?"

I spent a lot of time thinking about Lincoln and his depression. While I waited for one of my appointments, I read in an article by Joshua Shenk in *The Atlantic* that one of Lincoln's colleagues said the strongest element of his character was his "mysterious and profound melancholy." His law partner said of him, "His melancholy dripped from him as he walked."

My husband might say the same of me at times.

And yet, most of us learned about a very different Lincoln in school—the jovial Lincoln who was known for telling funny stories and having a quick wit, and who loved to visit with people in the White House.

My husband might also say this about me.

It is this juxtaposition of deep sadness, creativity, and an intense drive to connect with others that has always seemed like an ill-fitting puzzle for people who suffer from depression. And it's part of what made me erroneously decide I don't need medicine.

"Depression isn't me," I told myself. It was just something I went through once. It's not who I am.

Except it doesn't work that way. Diabetics often need medicine for the rest of their lives. So do people with heart disease. Likewise, depression is usually a lifelong condition. Often it is, in fact, part of who we are.

Several months later, I returned to the same hospital for a followup appointment. I was feeling better now, thanks to antidepressants, and it was like a curtain had lifted. I was out of my sweatpants, and I had curled my hair. I smiled at people. I was participating in the world again. I had come through to the other side, and I couldn't wait for my appointment to be done so I could get on with my life. I felt joy.

But I still think about the people I left behind in the waiting room, the ones whose curtains remain closed. That's the humbling part about depression. Once you've been through it, you know: We are all—Talbots dress or not—one crisis away from being in the waiting room, answering to one of "them" who won't look "us" in the eye.

I am still that person in the waiting room. So are many others. Depression is common in the military lifestyle. But it needn't be something that holds us back. It can be something that makes us grow.

As Shenk said of Lincoln in *The Atlantic* article, "Whatever greatness Lincoln achieved cannot be explained as a triumph over personal suffering … Lincoln didn't do great work because he solved the problem of his melancholy; the problem of his melancholy was all the more fuel for the fire of his great work."

Sarah Smiley is a Navy wife, syndicated columnist, and author of several books, including *Dinner With the Smileys* (Hyperion). Sarah believes depression isn't something of which to be ashamed. Instead, it provides moments of introspection, empathy, patience, and faith.

Where My Strength Comes From

Sara Horn

When you're a military spouse, people assume you are strong. Your civilian friends say "I don't know how you do it," as if there's an air of mystery or magic to getting your kids up for the day or dinner on the table when your better half isn't around to help.

Your spouse says "I know you can do it," as he or she rushes off for a quick formation or a long overseas deployment or one of those special temporary duty assignments that seem to have the glamour that life at home lacks—like maid service.

Your military spouse friends are more direct. They say, "You just do it." They already know you don't have a choice when your husband walks in with orders for a transfer, or that you don't get a vote when your wife gets called for sea duty. You are already in the club, and it's a strong club for strong people. There is no room for anything else. Strength is what helps the military family survive. Strength is what will help you survive.

So, yes, it's easy to assume you are strong when you're a military spouse. But it's much harder to admit when you are not.

Many months into our first deployment several years ago, I was tired from trying to do it all, weary from not sleeping, and exhausted from following the advice of everyone to "stay busy." I wonder how strength ever became equated with filling-up-every-hour-of-every-day-with-activity in the first place?

I sat on the couch in the middle of the day, the curtains pulled to ward off the sunshine, staring blankly at nothing in particular. The only thought at that moment running through my head was, "I'm done." But I knew I couldn't be.

Realizing it had been weeks, if not months, since I'd prayed, I sent out a desperate S.O.S.: "God, I'm so tired. I'm not strong enough. How can I keep going?"

In the silence of the room, as my tears fell, I felt God speak to me—not in audible tones, but through waves of reassurance to my heart. *You're not alone. You don't have to keep doing everything on your own. Let me be your strength.*

The realization was like a blindfold coming off. I suddenly saw so clearly all the ways I'd struggled to do everything myself, to control what I could and pretend to control what I couldn't.

I'd tried being everything to everyone—my husband's cheerleader, my child's nurturer, my friends' encourager. I had to admit, I'd come up quite short.

God's strength is so much greater than my strength. Holding on to my strength, my pride, and my own way wasn't working so well.

That day in the darkness of my living room, a pinpoint of light became more of a spotlight, shining brighter on a new understanding of what it looks like when I let God do the heavy lifting: I get out of the way and follow instead of insisting I lead.

There's a peace in remembering God is already in control and I don't have to be. I don't know what I would have done during that first deployment without my relationship with Christ. Six years and three deployments later, I'm grateful for the peace and the hope he continues to give me.

It's hard sometimes to trust what we can't see. It's even harder to believe in hope when hardship feels closer. But when we choose to trust God more than ourselves, we can depend on him to steady our hearts when uncertainty battles our minds. That's faith.

A scripture passage I've held onto for as many years as we've lived through deployments, is Romans 8:28: "And we know that in all things God works for the good of those who love him, who have been called according to his purpose." (*NIV*)

I've seen God work for my good in military life, whether through new friendships with other military spouses who encourage me, or new opportunities for me to encourage someone else. It's easy sometimes to focus on the hard stuff, the challenges, and the disappointments. But there are beautiful moments and gifts as well. I just have to look for them.

As my husband gets closer to retirement, and military life becomes a past season of our long life together, I know I will look back and see God's fingerprints everywhere. He touched our marriage when technology didn't cooperate and great distances stressed our communication. He touched our son who lived out half of his days between kindergarten and seventh grade with his dad being away and his mom trying to avoid being a crazy person. God touched our family, keeping us whole even when we were forced to be apart.

God also touched me. He helped me see that strength isn't

about what I can pick up, but what I'm willing to put down. He helped me understand that even in military life—maybe especially in military life—trusting him for each day gives me hope for the next.

He's the one who gives me hope, and only because of God, I can feel strong.

Sara Horn is a Navy wife and the author of multiple books, including *GOD Strong: The Military Wife's Spiritual Survival Guide* (Zondervan). The first of Sara's deployment experiences showed her the truest source of strength, and she's been sharing the message ever since.

Growing Our Family

Samantha Andrew

*M*y husband and I were on a painful journey through infertility when another military wife gave me a hug and whispered words of encouragement. She said she didn't know how God would bring a child into our lives— through adoption or birth—but she had faith our prayers would be answered and that one day she would cherish holding our baby while hearing our story.

Her kind words broke my frustration with people's unintended insensitivity and thoughtless words about our infertility struggles.

"When are you going to have kids?"

"Just stop trying, and it will happen; you're trying too hard."

Or my father-in-law's favorite: "You know something besides water comes out of the hose, right?"

Our story encompasses many heartbreaking attempts to have children over several years and three assignments. At year two of unsuccessful pregnancy attempts, we were stationed in Oklahoma. Our military primary care managers were supportive to the extent of the services they could provide: administer blood tests, write prescriptions, and refer us to a civilian infertility specialist.

The nearest specialist was a two-hour drive away, in Oklahoma City. TRICARE, our military insurance provider, would cover treatments for a civilian provider to determine the cause of infertility, but we knew TRICARE would not cover procedures intended to actively produce a pregnancy, such as artificial insemination and in vitro fertilization. We worked with civilian specialists for about a year, spending hundreds of out-of-pocket dollars for artificial insemination. We didn't know—and no one told us then—that there was also an infertility clinic at Wilford Hall, a major military facility less than a day's drive south of us at Lackland Air Force Base, San Antonio, Texas.

After a year of unsuccessful treatments, our specialists recommended in vitro fertilization. This option had a price tag of tens of thousands of dollars not covered by TRICARE, and a waitlist several months long. I went to my military primary care manager to get approval for the blood tests required to begin the IVF process and told him about our infertility progress. He told me about the military infertility clinic at Wilford Hall and offered to refer us there. The Wilford Hall clinic would provide IVF with no need to use TRICARE. If we had known the military even offered infertility clinics, we would have asked for that referral in the beginning of our process.

We immediately asked for a referral to Wilford Hall, and almost as immediately we received orders to move to California. We attended one appointment at the Texas clinic, and unfortunately, I did not take all my previous infertility records with me. The providers at Wilford Hall said they would have to begin our treatment from the beginning, assessing the reasons for our infertility. Meanwhile, we moved, and I began to research options for military care in California, closer to our new assignment. I discovered that Naval Medical Center in San Diego also offered an infertility program. I made an appointment with my new military primary care manager and asked for a referral to the San Diego clinic. After lengthy explanations of our infertility progress and the expenses we'd incurred, we received the referral as an Air Force couple to be seen at a Navy facility. We were seen within a few months. This time I hand-carried all my records, and because I provided documentation of our previous procedures and evaluations, we did not have to re-accomplish the many tests and procedures we had already been through. We were put directly on the two-year waiting list for in vitro fertilization.

Until that point, we had been completely focused on making a baby. The enforced waiting period allowed us to stop and ask ourselves if we wanted to face the physical and ethical implications of IVF. The procedure could potentially create more embryos than we could use. All those embryos would be our children, which created ethical concerns for us.

We had several friends with wonderful adoption stories; perhaps adoption was a better route. With our name on the IVF waiting list, we took advantage of the time and enrolled in our county's foster-to-adopt classes and completed a home study. Then we hit a complication familiar to military families: Our adoption counselor explained we could not relocate for more than three years after a baby was placed with us. We could not make that promise. The process stopped, and our hearts sank.

We started to ask God why he kept a longing for children in our hearts. By this point we were only six months into our two-year

IVF wait, yet a few days later we received news that an IVF slot had come open, and we were scheduled for the following month.

The entire process was completed on a San Diego military base and our doctors were all military; their understanding of our lifestyle and their guidance reassured us we were in the right place. While all fertility processes require complete dedication and adherence to a timetable to ensure proper treatment, shots, and ultrasounds at the right time within a fertility cycle, I never felt pressured. At the San Diego clinic, they understood my husband was active duty and that we had another challenge: The clinic was 300 miles from our home. The providers wrote non-descriptive orders to allow us to miss work for treatments without compromising our privacy. When my husband was away, they also offered to administer shots that he normally gave to me as part of my treatment.

In our first round, ten eggs were retrieved and fertilized. Only five survived through the five-day maturation. Two were transferred and implanted. At six weeks, blood tests confirmed the twin pregnancy, and my husband received short order notice for a six-month deployment. We did not fight the deployment, assuming he would return shortly before the birth. He left, and less than a week later I was rushed into surgery. That night I lost both babies at nine weeks and almost lost my own life due to a twin tubal pregnancy. My IVF team and my mom were with me through the surgery and recovery and assisted the Red Cross to get my husband home as soon as possible. He was home for ten days and then returned to his deployment. My IVF team monitored my physical and emotional well-being. Even with their support, I felt like someone had reached into my soul and ruptured all my hopes. I spent the next six months mourning the loss of our children.

When my husband returned from deployment, we timidly went back to San Diego for IVF round two. Two of the remaining embryos were transferred to my uterus but failed to implant. We were again devastated. I only had one embryo of hope left, yet I felt none. I finally prayed God would either place this baby in my arms or completely take away the desire to have a child forever.

Nine months after IVF round three, our beloved baby girl was born. She is our answer to prayer, a ten-year wedding anniversary gift from God. We thought she was destined to be our only child.

By the time our baby girl was one year old, we had orders again. We made a trip to San Diego to visit our IVF team and let them meet our daughter before we left. We explained that we planned to start the adoption process as soon as we arrived at our new location. Holding our baby, our IVF doctor told us of an unexpected opening in the IVF schedule. It was ours if we wanted it. We could be pregnant again before we moved. We accepted the offer as a gift from God. The medical team retrieved seven eggs, expecting only one or two would survive through the fertilization and growth stage. All seven survived. My husband was offered the rare opportunity to observe the miracle of life as he looked at the five-day old embryos under the microscope before they were transferred. They implanted successfully and eight months later, with no deployment and no complications, we delivered twins— our double blessing.

We now face the IVF ethical decision that held us at bay from the beginning of this journey. We have five healthy and strong embryos waiting to be born. We are on our third assignment in five years and have added a fourth child naturally—a gift after another deployment. I recently called my IVF team to discuss my remaining five embryos; we weren't sure if we wanted another pregnancy or not. They told me not to worry. The military has IVF teams in several locations and can make referrals and embryo transfers to wherever the Air Force assigns us. In addition, if we felt our family was complete, they could refer us to adoption agencies specializing in embryos. These agencies, like us, view each embryo as a child waiting to be born.

I remind myself often that we were given a beautiful story through the births of all of our children, and I pray the frustrations and struggles are never forgotten.

My friend who told me she looked forward to hearing the story of how a child came to be in our life received her answer when she held our precious first baby girl. This is the story she wanted to hear and the one I have longed to tell.

Samantha Andrew has been a military wife for almost twenty years and has four beautiful children. She chose to use a pseudonym to tell this story to protect her children's privacy and to honor Samantha and Andrew, two babies she loved and lost.

Loving My Sister

Briley Rossiter

*P*eople are put into our lives with a purpose. Some come to help us, others come to challenge us, and some people come because they need us. My younger sister, Ainsley, has come into my life for all these reasons.

I was only two years old when she was born. I remember thinking how amazing Ainsley was as a baby. Even then, I knew something was special about her, that she would change my life. I just didn't know how. Ainsley is beautiful, with wavy brown hair and mysterious gray eyes. But perhaps the most beautiful thing about Ainsley is her smile; it can brighten up a room better than any light bulb. Her smile is rare now and even more precious.

When Ainsley was born she appeared to be a normal baby. Nobody would have ever guessed that something was wrong, very wrong. She was reaching all of her milestones, saying simple words, crawling around, making messes, and eating almost everything she could reach. When Ainsley was fifteen months old, my mom became concerned that her baby was still not walking. She voiced those concerns with my dad, who was deployed to Iraq.

My dad is a United States Marine, and we were stationed at Camp Lejeune, North Carolina, at the time. So my mom took Ainsley to the doctor on base. The doctor said Ainsley had low muscle tone, which could be fixed with physical therapy. So,

Ainsley started seeing a physical therapist. Still, she didn't seem to be improving.

That was when it started: the research, the tests, the therapy, the trips to different hospitals and doctors. It took more than two years to find out what was wrong with Ainsley. I remember trying to wait patiently in the waiting room when I was six years old. I sat in a big chair in a room full of half-broken toys and books I'd already read. I was confused. I didn't know what was going to happen to my baby sister. Looking back, I realize that nobody did. None of us were prepared for her diagnosis.

My parents and the doctor were having a grownup talk in the corner while I sat next to Ainsley. The doctor gave my mom a small, folded piece of white paper and whispered something. Both of my parents nodded silently, and we left. When we got home, my parents unfolded the paper. Written on it, I would later find out, was "infantile neuroaxonal dystrophy." My mom and dad tried to explain it to me. I remember being very scared and confused.

Now I'm twelve, and those words are part of my life, because my little sister, Ainsley, has infantile neuroaxonal dystrophy, an extremely rare, genetic disease. Only about ten cases are known in the United States today. Most of us get rid of toxic substances in our bodies through exhaling and going to the bathroom. However, my sister's body contains a mutation that prevents her from disposing of these toxins. So they build up on her nerves and kill them, and over time, they will kill her, too.

As her nerves are destroyed, her brain loses the capability to spread information throughout her body. As the disease has progressed, Ainsley has lost the ability to walk, talk, and voluntarily control her limbs. Her muscles are extremely weak and almost nonfunctioning. She is losing her sight and her smile. In time, she will lose everything. There is no cure or treatment. Each day my family has to watch her slowly slip away from us. Ainsley's story has a predetermined ending, but her book has had the last page ripped out. Our family lives with an element of uncertainty.

When we received Ainsley's diagnosis, we had two options. We could crawl under a rock, feel sorry for ourselves, and waste the rest of our time with Ainsley, or we could continue moving forward with our heads held high, ready to overcome whatever obstacles life throws at us. We chose the second option.

We didn't want to let this disease become stronger than us. But it was still taking my sister from me. I couldn't do a lot of the things with Ainsley that I used to do with her. She could no longer have tea parties or play dolls with me. I knew we would never run and play together.

A few years after Ainsley's diagnosis, my dad got orders to Virginia Beach. Shortly after we were settled in Virginia, Ainsley's physical therapist introduced us to a local running group called Team Hoyt Virginia Beach. It was inspired by a father-son racing team from Massachusetts. The father, Dick Hoyt runs races while pushing his son, Rick, who is confined to a wheelchair. Together these two men have participated in thousands of races, ranging from five kilometers to marathons and triathlons. Mr. Hoyt pushes and pulls his son using special running and swimming equipment. Team Hoyt Virginia Beach helps children and adults with disabilities participate in races alongside able-bodied runners. They are pushed in a special running chair from start to finish. We were so excited when the physical therapist explained this to us, and we made plans to attend the next race.

Up to that point, Ainsley's life had been reduced to sitting on the sidelines. She went to all my dance recitals and to sports games to support our brother, Kamden, but she could only watch. This opportunity would change all that. Ainsley would be part of the race. For the first time in a very long time, Ainsley was finally able to go, to run, to roll with the wind.

It was clear that Ainsley loved running. When she felt the wind blowing on her face, she would light up and smile. First my dad pushed her in all the races, but soon I decided that I couldn't just watch anymore. I had to be out there, too. When I was nine, I became the youngest member of Team Hoyt Virginia Beach and began pushing Ainsley in races. Finally, we could do something together. It felt like we could be sisters again.

Ainsley's legacy is growing, and I'm blessed to be a part of it. Our aunt and our dad have created a nonprofit organization called Ainsley's Angels of America, which now has many sister organizations across the nation. These charities help other individuals with disabilities get the equipment they need to participate in races. They strive for inclusion and involvement with people of all ages and capabilities.

Another part of Ainsley's legacy is in print. A publisher asked my dad if he would be interested in writing a children's book about Ainsley's story. Of course he accepted, and he tried very hard, but failed. My dad is a Marine and he can do almost anything, but there's one thing he couldn't do, and that is write a book for kids. He tried to make it rhyme—not a good idea. I love him a lot, but I was not loving that book. About the time he was ready to give up, he asked if I would write it, and I did. *Born An Angel* is a picture book telling Ainsley's story.

Ainsley is not only my friend and sister, but also my inspiration. I'm going to be her legs and her voice because she can't use her own. I'm going to use my voice to shout her story from the top of the highest mountains because she cannot. I know, with all my heart, that this is a story that cannot die, and it won't. Ainsley's legacy will live on far beyond her numbered days.

Briley Rossiter is a Marine daughter, middle schooler, and published author. She has pledged all proceeds from her first book, *Born an Angel*, to Ainsley's Angels of America, an organization that assists America's special needs community in participating in endurance events. Briley believes in cherishing life's amazing breathtaking moments.

Rules of the Road Less Traveled

Jeremy L. Hilton

My family and I started down our less traveled road the day our first child, Kate, was born at Bethesda National Naval Medical Center. Until then, my wife and I had led a relatively charmed life: We both had successful military careers, a lovely little Cape Cod house, and a baby on the way. When Kate was born with significant medical issues, our lives changed forever. Reflecting back on the years since her birth, I've learned so much about a life I never knew existed. I am a better person, husband, and father because of a daughter who needs me to speak up for her and be her advocate.

In the neonatal intensive care unit where Kate spent the first four weeks of her life, we discovered the importance of advocating for our child. We learned a new language, suddenly talking about "bradycardia," "attendings vs. residents," and "DNRs." We learned that doctors know a lot, but parents are always the best—and sometimes only—advocates for our children. This lesson learned is one of the most important and it applies for the rest of our lives as parents.

Our little family spent the first five or six years of Kate's life simply surviving. Therapy, surgery, special education on one hand; PCSs, deployments, and training on the other. We were consumed with surviving each day. We experienced the good, the bad, and the ugly, making sure Kate had the best possible care in a mobile military life, not realizing those experiences were setting us up to become advocates for others. Once Kate's medical condition and our military life stabilized—relatively speaking—we realized we had the knowledge and ability to advocate for other families like ours.

Advocacy is speaking on behalf of those who can't speak for themselves. For my wife, Renae, and me, this means seeking improvements in the system that provides medical and educational intervention for special needs military children like Kate. I don't know if we made an impact in every situation. But at the very least, maybe we have made the system better for other military families.

Individual experiences prepare each of us to help others, whether making changes as a military spouse leader, or improving the community as an ombudsman, PTA member, or youth baseball coach. In any situation, advocating for others is an opportunity to make a positive impact.

On my journey of advocacy, I've learned a few things, which I've come to call my "Rules of the Road." For the record, I don't always follow my own rules—just ask my wife, friends, or certain members of Congress—but I'll share what I've learned about advocating in case it could help someone else:

Don't be a lunatic. Professional, thoughtful, and concise is the order of the day. There's a time and place for escalation, but it should not be the first step. Hone your message and then deliver it. Creating relationships is important, but the message is why you are there. You may get only a short time to deliver it. If it's a tough message, the person receiving it might love to talk about anything but the issue at hand. Hyperbole detracts from the primary message you are attempting to deliver.

Take everyone as they are. As advocates, we meet people where they are, not where we want them to be. We all have different skill sets. Appreciate everyone for what they're doing, not for what you want them to do. There are all different kinds of capabilities and different levels of support. Be thankful for any help a fellow military family member can provide without chastising anyone for not meeting a preconceived notion of what they should be doing. Be prepared when someone says "No." With that in mind, consider the next rule.

Learn to say no. Not every idea is a good one. I've learned that many times my first intuition about a person or an idea is often right. Learn to say "No" to a person or idea when necessary. In the advocacy world, you are guaranteed to make mistakes, but always remember that your reputation, particularly as it relates to trust, is the most important currency you can have. Saying "No" also helps maintain focus on what is essential. Being an expert in one policy area is better than being an amateur in two or three, which brings me to the next rule of the road.

You don't need to nor should you do it all. If your advocacy is for your own family—with your own healthcare providers or educators—and that's all you can do right now, then do what your family needs. Others might be at a different point, able to advocate outside their immediate family. Each should respect the other's situation. We'll all move in and out of various capability levels over time. When necessary, take a break or try something else. Your family and your military family need you around for the long haul. Don't get burned out.

Shine some light. When you meet fellow military spouses who want to learn or expand their repertoire, help them learn the ropes. You can't do it all, so allow the light to shine on other deserving spouses. We should be training the next generation of military family advocates. We certainly didn't get where we are without lots of support from the generations that came before us.

Nothing about us without us. The people who are affected by a decision or policy change should have a seat at the decision-making table. In bureaucracies, this concept is often overlooked. Whether in a spouses club, wing or battalion commander's meeting, or in the Pentagon, those most impacted by a policy should be included in the discussion. The decision may not always be in the advocates' favor, but their input should be considered. In the end, this is in everyone's best interest, because the decision or policy change will be better for getting the perspective of those who have the most at stake.

We are stronger together than we are apart. We forget this lesson far too often. We don't always have to agree at the tactical level, but when it comes to strategically advocating for military families, we need to keep this rule in the back of our collective heads. In the end, we need to find a way to support each other, even when we disagree.

Truly listening is such a gift, and we have so much to teach each other. Don't get hung up on differences of age, rank, or education.

Experience really does count for something, so listen when that senior spouse gives advice. You aren't obligated to follow their counsel, but I would recommend considering it. Likewise, many junior spouses are much more connected to what's happening on the ground and can provide insight on what really matters to today's military families.

Make your own "rules of the road." Not everyone will like this list. That's fine. Do what works for you. But get involved. Be an advocate. Please don't be silent. Our voices can make a difference.

Jeremy L. Hilton is a Navy veteran, Air Force husband, and advocate for military families, particularly those impacted by disabilities and chronic medical conditions. He was named Armed Forces Insurance Military Spouse of the Year in 2012 by *Military Spouse* magazine. He is an advisor to the TRICARE for Kids Coalition and the Military Family Advisory Network.

Coping With Serious Illness

Janine Boldrin

*W*hen my doctor called on a Sunday morning, I knew it couldn't be good news. I don't remember exactly what she said, but I do remember looking at my kids and my husband who were talking and full of smiles, unaware of what the doctor was saying in my ear. I walked back into the kitchen before I let myself sink to the floor, the phone still in my hand.

The test came back positive. I carried the same harmful gene mutation as my mother, the one that caused her to have both breast and ovarian cancer. My aunt and great-grandmother had both died from breast cancer around the age of forty, each leaving a young child behind. The test results confirmed I was at an elevated risk of getting breast and ovarian cancer at a young age, like my mom, my aunt, and my great-grandmother.

My mind went blank and I began to cry. As a military wife, I was used to worrying about my husband during deployment, but now I had to worry about whether I would be around to see our children grow up.

The phone call started a journey full of twists and turns. But right away, one of my biggest concerns was dealing with the complications that my husband's job in the Army would bring to the situation.

I thought there must be other military spouses who had
stumbled through this process before me. So I began talking
to friends and neighbors. Some had chronic conditions, others
were dealing with recent health issues, and all expressed the
same concerns that were running through my head. They talked
about a complex medical system and the fear that came with the
unpredictability of moves and deployments. If my family cancer
curse had taught me one thing, it was that any extra waiting or a
lack of good options could make a bad situation worse.

Military life means extra planning. Serious medical issues
demand more of the same.

Living far from extended family and the looming possibility of
deployments created a more complex puzzle. Could I find a good
doctor after our next move? Deployment departures and returns
are always fluid. How would I plan treatment and procedures
around them?

My doctors recommended a preventative mastectomy. Instead
of postponing the inevitable, I scheduled the surgery right away. I
had a ten-month old baby, so it wasn't the most ideal time for major
surgery. I wouldn't be able to lift or carry her during my recovery,
but I didn't want to put off the procedure only to have it bump up
against another move or deployment.

My early diagnosis was fortunate. I could choose the time and
place for the surgery, while my husband was home. Many military
spouses face unexpected illness or have a chronic condition
requiring treatment that has to happen during a deployment.
Receiving medical care is more challenging while living in a

remote location or when a spouse is deployed. When it comes to serious illness, some plans might need to change to accommodate treatment. End of story. Care should not be postponed longer than necessary. It may feel unfamiliar for a military spouse to be at the top of the family priority list, but that is what must happen in urgent cases.

Since my diagnosis, our family has gone through two moves, two deployments, and another baby. Along the way, I had a bilateral preventative mastectomy and now I go to specialists every six months to screen for ovarian cancer.

Before each move, I have to make sure there will be a doctor nearby who can treat me. Remote assignments were never at the top of our list, but the availability of an oncologist who can handle my case is now a part of our decision process. Usually, this means we need to be near a major city.

While being a military spouse has made our situation more complicated, I have also benefited from health insurance that covered the majority of my care, a community that stepped up to help me, and people willing to share knowledge they gained through their own experiences. I learned many things along the way.

I learned to be selective in what I share with others. Post-surgery was hard. I felt horrible for weeks and looked pretty bad. I was uncertain if I wanted people on our small installation to be asking me a lot of specific questions about my situation, but I also knew it would be hard to keep everything under wraps.

I had to decide early on how private or public I wanted to be about my medical issues. Military spouses want to rally around those in their community and, depending on your condition or your personality, this may not be what you want. Sometimes all the "help" can be overwhelming. In my case, I was careful with what I shared because the surgery was so personal.

We kept the people who needed to know—those who were closest to us—informed. I decided what I was willing to talk about and what I wasn't. When I was emotionally able to deal with questions, I told people more about what was going on. Now I feel totally comfortable sharing my story because I hope people can learn from my experience.

I found an insurance advocate. I needed personal support, and I needed professional advice as well. Treatment options can vary widely based on location. Insurance coverage can change from year to year. Because of this, it is essential to get the most up-to-date information available, not secondhand from a friend or a doctor's interpretation of insurance options.

Case management services through TRICARE, our military insurance provider, gave me a source of answers to many of my complex insurance and treatment questions. For anyone being treated for a chronic, high-risk, high-cost, catastrophic, or terminal illness, TRICARE offers free case managers who are usually nurses or social workers. My case manager knew how to dig for answers and could track all the voluminous paperwork involved in treating a serious condition.

Having an informed source is invaluable in unexpected situations. I was in the middle of the playground with two of my kids when I got a call from the pre-surgery consultant telling me the breast implants that would be used in reconstruction after my mastectomy would not be covered by insurance. Honestly, I can laugh about it now, but at that moment I felt confused and angry. I was emotionally exhausted from the months of planning and appointments.

Thankfully, my case manager was able to straighten things out with a phone call. She let the hospital know that TRICARE would cover the implants. She also laughed with me when I recounted telling the hospital representative that they could use tissues to fill me back up if it didn't work out.

I created a system to track my own paperwork. Even with a case manager, paperwork can be tedious and the phone calls seem endless, like running a marathon on top of illness, surgery, and recovery. To avoid total burnout, I began with a solid system in place right from the beginning for the medical care that would go on for months and even years. This means a complete paper trail including phone numbers to reach doctors, both past and present, notes about who I called and when, and what I learned from each conversation. For me, this means a binder—filled with phone numbers, authorization paperwork, and notes—that still travels with me to appointments.

Other paperwork included a copy of my will. We don't like to think about it, but both service members and spouses should have one.

I learned from my friends. Some of us are more private than others but talking to other military spouses about my situation, especially those who had been through similar experiences, was very helpful for both support and information. Some told me about the best doctors in the area, others gave advice about how to handle situations with TRICARE. Friends were also invaluable for help with childcare, meals, or a shoulder to lean on.

I turned to an online message board for people with the same gene mutation I have. I found other military spouses on the board who advised me to get a case manager through TRICARE. They discussed my options and pointed me toward the civilian specialist who did my surgery. These were women who could relate to what I was experiencing. Their advice was valuable as I came to bumps in the road or when I questioned if what I was doing was the right route for me.

I learned to let my husband take care of me. It's hard for me to let others take care of me, especially my husband. His work schedule and deployments mean I am in charge of the majority of stuff in our household most of the time. This is probably true for many military spouses, but sometimes we have to let go.

Post-surgery, I was pretty helpless for a while. It wasn't a feeling I had experienced before and was one I didn't like. But if I could find a bright spot out of that time, it was that my husband and I grew closer to each other. He became my caregiver, a role that confirmed I could rely on him when times were tough and I wasn't at my best.

You need a partner to help you. Early on, talk to your spouse about what you'll need from him or her to help you stay healthy. Become a team in your care.

Military families face many major life challenges with determination and hope. A medical issue should be the same. Keep pushing when things don't seem right, don't ignore that nagging voice telling you to get something checked or double checked, and turn to your best resources for help: your fellow military spouses and your own spouse. Then share your own story. What you say may be exactly what will help another military spouse through her journey.

Janine Boldrin is an Army wife and writer whose work has appeared in *The Huffington Post, Military Spouse,* and *Good Housekeeping.* Since her initial diagnosis several years ago, Janine has leaned on the wisdom of other military spouses and shares her story to help others navigate their medical journeys, too.

The Day Before the Wedding

Anna Alexander

*T*he police helicopter, looking like an angry black insect, came thundering into view, its wings chopping the air, the thwack-thwack-thwack reverberating off the hotel's stucco walls near which I huddled, trembling. With me was a young policewoman, the first of many officers I would see arriving in waves that day. I had called 911—the day before my son's wedding.

Inside the hotel was my son, a former Marine, angry beyond words, paranoid and delusional, and foaming at the corners of his mouth. He had been up all night and was under the influence of an illegal substance. In short, he was out-of-control. I was outside because he threatened to jump over the tenth story hotel balcony if I didn't leave.

Outside, wedding guests and waves of law enforcement officers arrived at the hotel. In one calamitous hour, the world had gone from sweet to horrible, and it was in this hour that my son's friends—most of whom I'd never met—came on the scene. Their mouths were open in disbelief, like the hundreds of other spectators witnessing this unfolding scene at the busy San Diego Harbor. This couldn't be happening.

As I provided vital information to the police about my son— height, weight, former military, bodybuilder—along with his mental status—post-traumatic stress, anger issues, high on drugs—

my husband's eyes locked with mine. How had we gotten here? What in the hell had gone so terribly wrong, so terribly fast?

Turns out it really hadn't been fast at all. The warning signs had been there all along, but the heat had increased slowly until it was boiling. Like the frog in the pan of water, we'd barely felt a thing until it was too late. When our son repeatedly struck out in anger over the years, we'd begun saying, "You know how he gets." We'd come to expect it and had learned to walk softly around him, without ever thinking about it. When our son openly smoked a drug known as "spice" at our home, he told us it was a synthetic cannabinoid and therefore harmless. I didn't even look it up. I took his word. Now I knew it was far from harmless.

As we stood outside the hotel together, an instantly-bonded group of people who love my son began telling frightening stories— ones we hadn't heard—all confirming what we now knew. This was serious. Inside the vortex of this drama, people I had met only moments earlier were now allies ready to help. The safety net had been formed, this band of brothers who vowed to keep two eyes on my son. Miracle number one had just occurred. In the midst of chaos, a loving and cohesive group emerged.

My son was taken into custody and sent to Balboa Hospital (Naval Medical Center San Diego) for a psychological evaluation and possible 72-hour hold. Inside the hotel, his bride-to-be knew nothing—yet. Would the wedding go on tomorrow? Would he be admitted, arrested, or released? We did not know. Outside the emergency room, we paced for four hours, down the same halls we'd paced when he was a child and sick, the same halls I'd paced alone when he had spinal surgery after a bomb exploded too near him in Iraq.

The intense effects of spice disappear rapidly. In the hours spent waiting for an assessment, he had returned to a calm state and was released. My husband and I felt beaten and bloodied. What would the wedding be like now? Would there be more problems? What about the reception, with the fuel of alcohol added to the fire? Would there be a scene? Were we even welcome?

The next day the wedding went on, but only after a couple of expletive-laced texts from my angry son. We all made it through the formalities, in spite of feeling like all the air had been sucked out of us. An outsider would never have known. No one would know from looking at the pictures. That was the second miracle.

We caught the first flight we could out of San Diego, where miracle number three occurred. In a city of millions, the blue-eyed blonde-haired officer who had walked me through the entire tragedy the day before the wedding was now working airport security. She wanted to know if the wedding had taken place. We were able to tell her it had, thank her, and then depart on the flight that would bring us home to begin the search for healing that our son so desperately needed.

I began with the Department of Veterans Affairs Crisis Line. From there I entered the amazing flow of caring people who guided me to where I needed to be: into a VA program called "Coaching into Care." I am learning what an intervention looks like and how to be the mother of an adult in this strange new land where all the rules are different. This opened the door to miracle number four.

Not only are my son's friends and family on the same loving page, but now the VA has guided me into a plan to help my son through his recovery when he is ready to seek help for himself. There is hope.

I still have a million fears: fear of losing my relationship with my son, his new wife, and our precious new granddaughter. I worry that we are 1,500 miles away and don't see how they are doing or how we might be able to help. I worry about interfering too much in their lives, or too little. I worry that we didn't intervene early enough. I just worry. I am out of my realm, but I've found help and support.

I wish I could stick my head in the sand. I wish it would all go away—out of sight, out of mind. But I can't. The journey is only beginning. I imagine the road will not be easy or follow in a straight line, but I pray that it will be what it is supposed to be and that there is a God who loves my son well and has already prepared the way.

For now, I look for gentle ways to stay engaged. Leaving him messages, letting him know we love him and feel his hurt. Expecting nothing, hoping for everything, and waiting for the next miracle.

Anna Alexander is the wife of a career Marine veteran and mother of an Iraq War veteran. After her son returned from battle, broken both physically and mentally, Anna embarked on a search to find—and be—the support he needs. She writes under a pseudonym to protect his privacy and hers.

Bread of Sorrows

Grief

———————— ··· ~ ··· ————————

"All sorrows are less with bread."
~ Miguel de Cervantes Saavedra

Secondary Losses

Artis Henderson

The military calls them secondary losses—all the hurts we don't see coming when someone we love is killed in combat. After my husband, Miles, died in a helicopter crash in Iraq in the fall of 2006, I thought I knew what they meant: the severing of my ties to the Army, the falling away of a community, the end to a way of life that had given structure and meaning to my days. All this I saw coming. What I did not see then, and am only seeing now, is the loss of children we never had.

When Miles and I were first dating, we often said flippantly that we didn't want kids. We were so wrapped up in each other, so enmeshed in our plans for the future, that we could not imagine what place children would have in the life we were creating. We thought we would travel widely, experience rash adventures, and live the sort of lifestyle where kids would only get in the way. And we were young. He was twenty-four when he died; I was twenty-six.

A year and a half after Miles's death, I made friends with two other military widows who were also childless. We were close in age, but I was the youngest by three years. For me, the issue of children had not yet started to sting. I was too early in my grief, too bowled over by the immediacy of Miles's absence. I had trouble thinking beyond the next day. One of the widows told me that she and her husband had planned to start their family when he was home on R&R from Afghanistan. He was killed before he made the mid-tour break.

"Now," she said, "I don't hold babies."

I hurt for her without fully understanding what she meant.

Then my best friends, women my age, started having children, and it occurred to me with a clench of regret that if Miles had lived we would be talking about starting our own family. Soon, the subject of children began to make me ache. My mother-in-law took me to a baby shower where the mom-to-be held a bib over her round belly, and I thought I would crumble. At get-togethers with friends, I started shaking my head when they tried to pass me their babies. I found I could not hold them. I turned thirty, then thirty-one. A good friend who is single and without children began having irregular periods. She went to see her doctor, who ran some tests and discovered that a key hormone was dropping. If she planned to have children, the doctor said, she needed to begin soon. My friend told me this news over the phone and we were quiet together, and sad together, because we knew both our windows were closing.

Now I am thirty-three and childless, in a way, by choice. I know there are options out there for women like me, but I wonder if that would be missing the point.

Last summer I took a trip to Ireland with my two widowed friends. We stayed at a bed and breakfast along the Antrim Coast, in the north part of the country, where on a clear day you can see across to Scotland. Our host, Ernie, was in his early seventies, a widower, charming, and dapper. He ran the inn as a hobby, he told us, but he'd never had three single women there before. He seemed delighted at his luck, if perplexed. How could we be unmarried and without children? One morning at breakfast he came into the dining room and stood smiling with his hands on his hips, taking us in. The day was bright and sunshine spilled across the table. Through the bay windows, the sea glittered.

"Look at you," Ernie said, beaming. "You would make such wonderful wives. I can just see you now, there at the table, your children running about the room."

I had to turn my face away so he would not see me weep.

Late that afternoon, at a pub in town, I confessed to my friends that I was considering having a baby on my own. They weighed the idea carefully. Was I the type of woman who could raise a child alone, they asked? Was I prepared financially? Emotionally? These were the questions I had been asking myself. Eventually the conversation worked its way around to paternity. Who would father this baby?

I suggested an old friend.

"Is he married?" one of my friends asked.

I nodded. He is.

She shook her head. "That would be complicated."

We were silent for a time, turning over the options. A rugby match played on a screen behind the bar, its volume turned low. Quietly, my friend voiced what each of us was thinking.

"It's not that we want babies," she said. "We want our husbands' babies."

Artis Henderson is an Army widow, author of *Unremarried Widow* (Simon & Schuster), and a journalist whose work has appeared in *The New York Times* and *Readers Digest*. Military widowhood comes with many losses; Artis is grateful not to have counted her Army family among them.

Living for Griffin

Kristine Schellhaas

When I imagined telling my husband that we were pregnant with our first child, I did not envision it happening over the phone while he was in Iraq. I never thought I'd be lugging myself to the store at midnight to buy pickles and ice cream. I thought my husband would be there to lovingly rub my feet or my back as we awaited the birth together. Instead I found myself alone.

I'm not going to lie. I got jealous when I saw the cozy lives my non-military friends were living. They had great careers. They were busy buying homes, celebrating special moments together, enjoying pregnancies and childbirth as couples, and relishing the reprieve when friends and family swooped in when they needed help.

My life was complicated in more ways than one. My Marine was fighting back-to-back wars. When he was home, he was busy training. I was the one who became a zombie, sleep walking through the night with one crying baby—then another. I alone had to clean up after the child who had pooped in the tub (again!) and had to mentally prepare myself for my own hellish brand of combat for a simple trip to the grocery store with two little ones.

The truth was that I had an absentee husband, not because he didn't care but because he was busy serving our country. Life was tough enough on those terms, and with young kids in the mix it was more difficult.

My boys meant the world to me, and seeing the world through their eyes was truly amazing. Their innocence, joy, and enthusiasm for life were infectious. I loved our little Griffin and Quaid more than anything, but I remember saying several times, "I'm not happy," because I was living a life I had never envisioned for myself. The stress and chaos were often overwhelming. I was thousands of miles away from my family, from support, from any sense of personal fulfillment outside the title "Mom."

I thought I knew what unhappiness was. But I didn't. Not yet.

After less than a year at Fort Benning, Georgia, we had recently moved to a small isolated base on the other side of the country: Twentynine Palms, California.

Our boys, Griffin and Quaid, were about to turn one and three, so we went to San Diego for the weekend to celebrate both their birthdays. It was a place that felt a little more like home since my father-in-law had recently remarried, and we gained new family in the area.

When I got ready to go shopping for their birthday party, I hesitated about leaving our youngest son, Griffin. He was a busy little guy and required a lot of attention. I was torn between taking him with me and being slowed down, or leaving him behind so that my husband could get a heavy dose of single parenting. In the end, I chose the latter.

As I drove back home with party supplies in hand, I received a phone call that forever changed everything. It was my husband. He said, "Griffin fell in the pool. He isn't breathing." As he finished saying these words the cell connection was lost. There was nothing. I was numb. My world moved in slow motion except for my frantic, dialing fingers.

I tried to call him back. But there was no answer.

My mind raced. *How could this happen? Is Griffin okay? Why wasn't anyone watching him? I shouldn't have left him behind. I should have been able to trust family.* I wouldn't know anything for the next thirty minutes, until I pulled into a cul-de-sac overflowing with fire trucks, ambulances, and police cars.

My husband ran to me. I screamed and shoved him as hard I could. I was weeping uncontrollably; all I wanted to know was whether or not Griffin was okay, and *how this could happen?* He hugged me close and cried with me, saying that he had left Griffin in the care of my in-laws so he could set up the portable crib for the night. In the few short minutes my husband was busy, Griffin crawled undetected to the bedroom where the dog opened the door with his paw and went outside. Griffin followed. My husband found him in the pool only moments later, but it was too late.

I rushed toward the ambulance. I could barely see my son through my tears, through the mask that covered his face. He was there, but not really. The paramedic was performing CPR, trying to bring him back.

All I could do was think about my beautiful little boy. He was a child who rarely cried—so full of life, so full of smiles. He was the one who stopped adults in their tracks with his stunning blue eyes and wispy blonde hair.

We all stood in the cold waiting, watching for any sign of

change. It had been too long. I knew something was wrong. Finally, a helicopter transported him to Rady Children's Hospital.

We quickly followed in our car. When we walked through the hospital doors the staff immediately recognized us, though we'd never met before. They hurried across the lobby and escorted us to the back, where they told us our son had passed away. We were then led to a private room to say goodbye to our perfect little boy.

The next morning, we loaded our oldest son into the car to drive back to Twentynine Palms—without our beloved Griffin. Quaid couldn't understand why his best friend wasn't in the car seat next to him. "Where's Griffin?" he asked. "Where is brother? We need to go find him."

It was the first of many difficult conversations, explaining that his baby brother was going to be watching us from the heavens.

When we arrived home, my grief consumed me. I wanted to shut down, to disappear.

During the weeks and months that followed, I played the destructive "what if" game. I couldn't help it. *What if we had never received orders to Twentynine Palms? What if we had never gone to San Diego? What if I hadn't left Griffin behind that morning? What if I hadn't married my Marine?*

The trail of what-ifs led me down a spiraling black hole of negativity. One true string connected me to the world: my only remaining son, Quaid. I knew I needed to stay strong for him. If I didn't, I feared I would lose him, too.

Six months later, my husband deployed again—this time to war in the Helmand Province of Afghanistan, where he and his fellow

Marines would face one of the worst conflicts the Marine Corps experienced in Operation Enduring Freedom.

We had discovered that we were expecting another child shortly before my husband left. I gave birth to our beautiful baby girl while he was away fighting, and I realized while holding her in the hospital, I needed to stop the "what-ifs" and start celebrating life again.

Before we lost our son, I was waiting for happiness to come to me, but it never felt possible because I felt I couldn't accomplish my dreams and goals in our military lifestyle. I couldn't choose where we lived. I couldn't have the career I wanted because of all the new orders and subsequent moves. I didn't even have a regular, daily routine in my own home because of my husband's irregular schedule.

I knew I needed to change my perspective and find a way to care about life again. That meant I had to find happiness with what I had, and I needed to stop blaming others for what had happened. I had to accept that losing Griffin was a terrible, awful accident.

I was being selfish by focusing on my own grief—so much so that I couldn't stop and consider that my husband was hurting, too. He had been there at the house that day. He was the one who had to pull Griffin out of the pool. There was nothing in the world I could project onto him that could be worse than the looping guilt and self-disappointment echoing endlessly in his heart and mind.

Now he was in Afghanistan and losing his Marines to war. Each time he wrote a letter to a fallen Marine's parents, he too bled: he knew what it was like to lose a son. I thought about our marriage, about everything we faced together in life. I reconsidered the wedding vows we had exchanged before friends and family. I had a really big reason to leave—all this pain—but I had a million reasons to stay.

As I began to search for my own happiness, I started making changes. The first thing I did was cut out negative relationships. I no longer had sympathy or patience for caustic people or for those who complained constantly.

When my husband returned home, we struggled to find adequate counseling in our area. After a long search, we finally found someone we could talk to. Counseling didn't heal us, though. We used the process to create a makeshift Band-Aid over our hearts to help us get through without Griffin. Our healing had to come from changes made within.

I knew from experience that the Marine Corps wasn't going to change, so I learned to be like water, to move with the ebb and flow of our lifestyle. I leaned in, I embraced my military community. I started celebrating accomplishments and small moments more than I ever had before. I looked for what really mattered in life. In the end, I discovered I had a choice. I began to choose to be happy.

That choice has never been easy, and some days I struggle with my outlook. Part of me knows that we will never fully heal, even though we've come to terms with our loss. As time goes by, the pain diminishes and we remember the good times with Griffin— his smile, his eyes, his sweet nature. But in truth, there's nothing more we can do now. He is gone. We must let him go, and that's a constant struggle. We live day by day as best we can.

So now I wrestle for my happiness. I remember how scared and confused I felt when receiving orders to duty stations I knew nothing about, so I set out to help others navigate military life. I started a website designed to inspire, connect, and educate other military families, with the hope that they too, could realize a happier military life. I discovered that focusing my energy on helping others takes the focus off my own hurt and despair. Through these actions, I forge peace with my circumstances.

I also knew that I didn't want to be known as the woman who had lost her child. I wanted to be known as someone who paved the way for others. As I have said, it's neither easy nor automatic. But that doesn't mean it isn't worth it.

It's been six years now. I think about our son daily.

This is difficult to write, because I will never truly heal from losing him. There's still a Band-Aid over my heart that helps me get through life, and sometimes it's ripped off. But I'm done feeling sorry for myself. It's how we react to the adversity we face in life that makes us become who we really are. All I can do now is encourage others to dare greatly, to do the things that my son never got a chance to do.

That's what I'm doing.

I'm living for Griffin.

Kristine Schellhaas is a Marine wife and the founder of USMC Life, an organization that informs and connects Marine Corps families. Kristine refuses to allow her hardships to dictate who she will become, but instead uses her strength to uplift those around her as a motivational speaker and author.

Star Light, Star Bright

Karen Pavlicin-Fragnito

"Red sky at night, sailors' delight." I position my camera to take in more of the sky as the rhyme plays in my head. Tomorrow will be a good day.

The Minnesota sky often reminds me of food. Tonight is rainbow sherbet with a swirl of strawberry shortcake. Tonight's clouds reach far and wide and up and up, creating a view too enormous to fit in my lens.

Grief is like that, too—enormous. It goes beyond what I can see.

I bring the camera down to the daisies and zoom in. I love the way the late sun backlights the petals. This is the flower garden Alexander and I planted when we installed the flag pole in honor of his daddy. We made our own walking stones to create a path. This one says, "Love you to the moon and back."

I sit on the porch listening to kids play in a nearby cul-de-sac. Our street is quiet tonight; most of the kids are teenagers now.

Alexander's daddy made the Adirondack chair I sit in. I rest my hand on the arm and consider the construction; loosening one screw allows the chair to collapse to be stored in winter. He had a gift for creative woodworking.

It is easier for me to think of Bob as Alexander's daddy than it is to call him my husband. Just as it is easier to say he's dead than it is to talk about what I loved about him or how wonderful our marriage was. It's more painful to remember the joy, the reasons I miss him. It's the good stuff that makes me cry. And laugh. And catch more tears in my throat. Joy is the crux of grief. Did I mention it's enormous?

Bob, known as "Fightin' Bob" to his battle buddies, proudly served as a Marine. He came home safe from multiple deployments, two helicopter crashes, and being handed a booby-trapped grenade. We thought he was invincible.

When he was diagnosed with stage four colon cancer, every person who knew him was confident he would beat it, statistics be damned. He outlasted his prognosis, renewing our hope and faith.

But he was not invincible.

Alexander was turning four years old at the time, and he was intensely aware of the situation. He peeked his head through our bedroom door that dark Sunday morning and said, "I think we should all be together." I put my arms out and he climbed up into my lap and reached over to his daddy. "Don't be afraid, Daddy," he whispered. "God will carry you on his lap and bring you up to heaven."

In the days following Bob's death, Alexander had lots of questions about heaven. "Can Daddy hear us even if we don't say anything?" "Where do they sit when there are no clouds?" "Do souls have teeth?"

A month after Bob died, a grief counselor walked with Alexander around our home. In each room they entered, she asked him what was the same and what was different now that his dad was gone. Alexander slept in the same bed in the same bedroom.

Comfort. He still ate dinner at the same table in the same kitchen, but now Daddy's chair stayed empty. *The Ultimate Deployment,* I thought.

We created new routines, new holiday traditions, Mommy-Alexander days. We traveled together, hiked together. On special days, like Father's Day and Bob's "heaven birthday," we sent messages from this front porch up to that big sky via helium balloons.

I checked new boxes on medical and school forms: widow, single parent.

It took me two years to gather the strength to go through Bob's clothes to donate them. When I did, there was a pair of jeans that still smelled like him. More time passed before my memory stopped replaying scenes of his last days and allowed stories of our friendship to resurface.

New adventures, such as Cub Scouts, reminded Alexander that his daddy was too far away to go on campouts or build Pinewood Derby cars. It takes a village. Uncle Dave joined him on the first overnight campout. Our neighbor became his Akela—they won grand champ of the Pinewood Derby every year.

I gained thirty pounds, lost twenty-five, gained ten more. Gave in to reading glasses. The house was struck by lightning. I was attacked by a swarm of yellowjackets. We replaced the furnace, painted the kitchen, and said goodbye to PaPop and Granpop, who joined Bob in heaven.

One day, I accidentally hung the flag upside down in the international sign of distress.

My extraordinary relationship with Bob eventually encouraged me to find love again. On this front porch, I introduced ten-year-old Alexander to Geno. He thought it would be cool to have both a heaven dad and an earth dad.

Geno's two daughters took longer to warm up to the idea of a stepmom, first scripting a sequel to *The Parent Trap*. We later graduated to our own version of reality TV: *Newlyweds With Teens*.

Blended families are built on a foundation of grief: marriages cut short, more complicated technicalities for defining the word *related*. Joy in new relationships doesn't change how much you miss the old.

Now fifteen, Alexander looks and acts more and more like Bob every day. They have the same smile, the same sense of humor and *carpe diem*, love of God, and fearless dancing. Family, friends, and faithful Marines all keep Bob's stories alive. Alexander's own memories are a mix of senses and images. He thinks of his dad when he hears certain songs they listened to together. He remembers playing the car racing video game and dancing to the Beatles. He remembers the morning his dad died. Mostly, he remembers a feeling of love.

I look up at the enormous sky once more. The moon appears. Far enough away to measure love, close enough to bridge heaven and earth. A star shines through.

"Star light, star bright, first star I see tonight, I wish … " the rhyme begins in my head.

The front door opens. I hear our teens laughing, Geno teasing. It's time for ice cream.

I leave the wish in the sky for someone else—someone who hasn't already had everything.

Professionally, **Karen Pavlicin-Fragnito** is an award-winning writer, international speaker, and accomplished business leader. But on her front porch, she's a wife, mom, stepmom, and neighbor. She loves to sing, travel, and take pictures of the Minnesota sky.

A Piece of (Wedding) Cake

Military Marriage

··· ~ ···

"I'll have what she's having."
~ Lady at the diner, When Harry Met Sally

Marriage Pig Latin

Lori Volkman

*W*ild-eyed, clinging children were being ripped from their mothers' arms; a puddle of questionable origin pooled in the backpack-unpacking zone, and a flurry of focused work-bound parents avoided the mess while encouraging their five-year-old dawdlers to "hurry up" for the forty-ninth time in fifteen minutes.

Kindergarten hallways are not for the faint of heart, and I now accept full responsibility for failing to adequately prepare my husband. But this man had seen combat. He could handle kindergarten.

For me, the trek to the classroom was familiar. I followed directly behind the kids. But when I finally arrived at the classroom door and turned to introduce Randy to the teacher, he was standing flush against the wall looking at me like he'd rather be in an underwater cage, bleeding ever so slightly and encircled by starving sharks.

But he wasn't. He was home. After a fifteen-month deployment, he was navigating the crowd at an elementary school so he could meet his children's teachers.

We did introductions quickly and headed for the third grade hallway. As we walked, Randy had this weird smile pasted on his face. I didn't realize it at first, but people who passed us were giving him the surprised, open-mouthed, "Well, hi there!" smile as he passed them in the hallway. He managed an occasional, "Ha ha, good to see you too," and an, "Oh, uh, thank you," but otherwise just nodded and smiled stiffly. One woman he didn't know hugged him, and some of them hugged me. One even raised her hands to cover her mouth as if she were going to cry.

"I've been praying for you!" she blurted out.

I looked at my husband's pasted smile. He looked a little too much like a scarecrow, friendly, but scary.

When we finally arrived in the third grade hallway, we did the same quick introduction drill as the bell rang. The hallway was empty now except for some jogging students and moms considering skipping their workouts for coffee dates.

I felt my husband's hand on my back. It was so nice to have it there. But then I felt the pressure increase. I was suddenly leaning forward as I walked, his hand propelling me forward. I realized it was not there for affection. It was for acceleration.

Down the hall, I saw a friend. Randy leaned forward to whisper in my ear, "Keep going. Don't stop." As we closed in, I tried to avoid being smashed by the weight of his urgency and still smile at my friend. He almost ran into me when I felt compelled to stop. As I turned to him, the look on his face burned into me the full weight of disobeying a direct order. My friend laughed at our two stooges shenanigans.

"Welcome home!" she said.

I attempted to explain away my buffoonery, blurting out something relatively incomprehensible about Randy getting hugged by strangers and not recognizing anyone, because he didn't actually know anyone, but maybe he thought he should know people but not including her of course, and I didn't mean her, I meant this other woman that randomly hugged him, and how it was really good to have him home and it was the first time we had really gone anywhere and, you know ... I trailed off.

She smiled. I smiled. The Scarecrow smiled.

After an awkward silence, we returned to the car. I wondered what had just happened.

"What's wrong?" I asked, not knowing if I wanted the answer.

"I didn't realize I'd be seeing people here."

"People? Like, do you mean, as in, parents?"

This conversation was getting dumb, and getting there fast.

"Well, that is what happens in the morning. Parents drop off their kids. Who did you think was going to be here?"

"We were supposed to meet teachers."

"We did."

"There were other people. I didn't shave."

He said it matter-of-factly, as if I should have known he didn't want to walk into any scenario without the appropriate briefing. It made me want to laugh hysterically and cry all at the same time. I couldn't believe he was serious, but he was. Dead serious. I was confused.

And at that moment, I realized it: After a year and a half apart, we were officially reintegrating. This post-deployment process of putting a relationship back together is harder than deployment. There, I said it out loud. Homecoming isn't the magic pill that cures deployment.

Four months later, my confusion turned into something else. It wasn't the loneliness I felt during Randy's deployment, but it was the kind of lonely you can feel in a crowded room full of strangers.

I was staring at my long-legged sleeping son who had crawled in bed with me, and I started to think about what it must feel like to have missed things that can never be reclaimed. My husband was on another trip. A short one, but he was gone, missing another holiday.

I looked down at my cell phone, and my fingers typed out the first thing that came to my mind: "I can't remember the last time you were home for Easter. That can't be good." Send.

It was dispatched across the Pacific Ocean. I couldn't take it back.

I flopped my head down on the pillow, trying hard to recall our Easters past, rubbing the little ankles that had sprawled over to my side of the bed. The phone buzzed, interrupting my thoughts.

It said one thing: "Sorry."

He couldn't remember, either. I put the phone away. I couldn't muster a follow-up.

He'd be on a training exercise while I sat through the Easter service, admonishing my kids not to snicker at the lady with the big purple hat. He'd be in a windowless room for twelve hours while I smiled at children scrambling mercilessly over each other in search of eggs. He'd return to musty quarters eating a commissary snack out of a plastic dish about the time I prepared for a houseful of friends, the smell of rosemary filling the room, the sun flooding my kitchen with yellow light. He was the one missing everything, not me. I wasn't alone, but I was still lonely.

So I worked a lot during that time.

And my job wasn't that soothing, either. As a deputy prosecutor, one of my duties was to advise officials like the sheriff about which documents to release in high-profile cases. I often had to look at some pretty nasty crime scene photos. So there I was the following week, working late and flicking through glossy photos, bracing myself for the ones I had been prewarned about by the investigator. I definitely didn't feel lonely. I felt sweaty.

After I got through it, I went to happy hour. That seemed like the right thing to do: Be happy. I called my longtime law school friend, a former district attorney who always makes me laugh until I cry by saying completely inappropriate things like "douche nozzle" just a smidgen too loud in public places.

Kelly took one look at me and said it right away: "Are you okay?" I wasn't. Kelly Walsh comes from a big family of Irish Catholics in Montana, and she doesn't take anything fake from anybody without calling them out on it. So instead of lying to her, I raised my glass for an air-clink. She hugged me before settling into the chair next to mine.

Without looking up, I told her I'd been looking at crime scene photos for three hours, and she nodded. She knew exactly what I meant, and she wasn't about to ask questions. Likewise, I knew not to share the details, because those are the kinds of things that can infect you. You want to share, because it feels like it might somehow purge your memory. You learn quickly that it doesn't. Plus, I knew she had her fair share of images indelibly marked on her own soul. We talked about everything else for the next two hours.

When I finally got home, Randy walked into the kitchen and found me seated at the table with a bottle of red wine and a glass. I wasn't drinking it. I was just staring at it, remembering the day that I poured an entire bottle down the garbage disposal after finishing a particularly sickening case, because I had turned to wine ten consecutive nights in a row. Randy grabbed another glass, poured himself one, and sat down. "So what's going on?"

That shocked me a little.

Over our twenty years of marriage, when I've come home in a work-induced foul mood, he has traditionally and successfully taken the "ignoring it until it goes away" strategy. But yet, here he was, sipping wine and looking at me. It completely disarmed me.

I started talking. I told him about the bad man. I told him about the child, the blood, and the dead body. I purged what I shouldn't have. I told him about the interrogation and the police report and the autopsy. And then I told him the part that was bothering me. I told him the part that got to me.

"Her hands looked just like Olivia's."

Our daughter has very distinctive hands. Her father's hands. I buried my face, sobbing. A day's worth of tension came out all at once. All the light-speed photo flipping, the small talk from happy hour, all the distracting office chit-chat. It all fell down at once.

He sat very still across the table from me as I sobbed. He didn't move. When I stopped crying, he spoke. "I can't tell you details, but I know how you feel. You have to get someone else to look at those photos, someone who doesn't have kids."

I watched him as he got up from the table to go back to whatever he had been working on before finding me with my wine bottle. I felt empty when he walked away without hugging me, and I wished that affectionate part of him would come back soon. But I knew this wasn't theoretical advice. Our experiences overlapped.

It felt like connection.

Post-deployment reintegration turns out to be a two-steps-forward, one-step-back kind of thing. And in the movement back and forth, it starts to feel a little like a familiar dance. It's klutzy and outdated, and a lot of toes get stepped on—until the footing beneath starts to become common ground.

One of my most difficult struggles with reintegration was not stepping forward all the time. I tried my hardest to find a way to give Randy the space he needed. I was very understanding about it.

"Space!? You just had fifteen months of space, Jackwagon!"

Believe me. I knew how to create space.

This idea of giving him space really offended me when it dragged on into the sixth and seventh month after his return. He describes it now as a scab I kept picking at mercilessly, peeling it off before what was underneath had completely healed.

I began feeling horribly insecure. I stood in front of the mirror wondering what in the world was wrong with me. I tried being nicer (fake). I tried being a supermom and super wife (exhausting). I tried being demanding (annoying). I tried twice-a-day workouts and a vegan cleanse (cranky). I even tried being funny, which actually worked for me from a mental health standpoint, until I realized I was the only one laughing. Then it was just sad.

The bottom line is that I tried everything, and everything I tried created even more space between us. As the months rolled on, my husband seemed to be getting further and further away.

Enter, the hookah.

That's a big shisha pipe that looks a lot like you're about to smoke some weed. Deputy prosecutors are not typically found in "smoke shops," yet here I was, shopping for a hookah. This was something he had occasion to do Over There. This was something he enjoyed doing with his other friends. This was what he wanted.

The winning model wasn't a modest table-top variety, either. It had to be the big five-foot-high, four-hose contraption with colored glass and velvet tubes and rich wooden handles. It barely fit into our car.

For several months it gathered dust, and so did I. I started coming home each night in a daze. I fixed dinner, managed what little housework I could stand, loved on my kids, and went to bed. I quit staying up late, quit waiting for him to come to bed, and quit wandering into his office to see what he was up to. I quit lingering near him waiting for a kiss. I quit asking him about his day. I quit volunteering to tell him about mine.

It just sort of happened. Space happened.

And then Randy starting polishing that hookah. I came home to find him assembling it, checking the seals, igniting the coals, packing gooey sweet fruit-flavored shisha into a ceramic bowl and filling the psychedelic glass bulb with hot water. I joined him on the deck, surprised by his level of conversation and engagement with me, and took my first reluctant suck of the foreign-smelling tube which was sure to cause me to lose my job and my dignity. And I choked.

But as we sat there, the smell got sweeter, and I learned to go slowly. I breathed in the melon tobacco and let it soak into my senses. I watched my husband as the smoke curled around his lips. He seemed to release more than simply a breath. As the sun set and my husband's feet brushed against mine, he leaned back in his chair, golden light shining in his eyes. He told stories without that faraway stare, not reminiscing so much as sharing.

And he smiled. His shoulders dropped into a comfortable curve. Pretty soon there was a chill, and we wrapped up in blankets and quilts, and he pointed out the rising moon. It was like time stood still for a little while. We joked about what the neighbors could see and whether the girl who sold us the contraption laughed when she saw us leaving with it. And I looked over at him.

"What was it like? Is this similar to what you had over there?"

"Yeah, pretty much. I'm glad you like it. Not everyone does."

"Why did you like it so much?"

"It was one of the only times we really relaxed."

"Relaxed?"

"When we worked, we were scrambling. The idea of sitting for hours was a luxury. The idea alone was relaxing. Of course it was also still 100 degrees in the evening over there, so doing it from underneath a blanket is a little different."

We both chuckled, and he flashed a smile. The space between us seemed to disappear. After ten months, the space was finally starting to go away. It was the beginning of the end of reintegration.

We hadn't been on a real family vacation since before the deployment. After Randy had been home as long as he had been gone, and with the help of accumulated air miles, we booked a trip for four to Mexico. We still sucked a little at talking to each other over prolonged periods of time, so after the first two days, I found myself talking with the locals I had access to: taxi drivers, wait staff, bartenders, hotel maids, and beach vendors. And I loved it.

Randy had spent a portion of his childhood in Germany, following his mother through the opera houses of Europe in the early part of her opera career, ingesting the language so fully that by the time he was eight, school children there couldn't even tell he was an American.

In contrast to his erudite Euro-enlightenment via opera houses, I misspent a good portion of my late childhood following the high school skippers from sixth period right across the border into Tijuana, where I managed to ingest many things other than the language. I somehow learned some Spanish along the way. And so in Mexico, I proudly did the talking. About three days into the trip, I started to remember vocabulary and conjugation.

Emboldened, I decided to use Spanish on the very next person I saw on my way to beachside yoga. An elderly Mexican woman in a gauzy cream-colored top and pants walked rather slowly in my direction, so I unleashed the full extent of my Spanish greeting prowess upon her: *"Buenos dias. Que tenga un buen dia!"*

My tan and my accent must've been much better than I realized, because this woman I didn't know was suddenly explaining, in what appeared to be relatively graphic detail, the terrible or wonderful story of the injury or illness or surgery or table-dancing incident or debilitating disease she suffered from, which afflicted her knee or hip or bellybutton or right temple when she was in her youth or three days or two years ago, which caused her to move slowly or dance less or stub her toe this morning.

I panicked when I heard the inflection in her voice shift to that flick you can sense at the very last part of a sentence, the telltale sign that a question was coming. "I don't actually speak Spanish," I finally said in English.

And there we stood smiling stupidly at each other, not knowing what to do next. We needed a translator, but it didn't feel like it was worth it. It was easier to nod and walk toward yoga in silence. It was easier to wonder what she said, to make it up based on what I thought I heard.

At the end of yoga, I laid with my eyes closed, listening to the waves and feeling the heat push into my skin as the day warmed up. I could hear the voice of the yogi floating around from student to student, admonishing us to clear our minds and think of nothing, and I was very near a dream-like state as the waves roared. That deep percussive pounding of the ocean is the glue that sticks my Navy childhood together. There's something about the way it vibrates that feels like the sound comes from inside me. It swells, deep and introspective. I breathed in deeply, and my subconscious conjured my husband. We were standing on the path facing each other, right where I'd been facing the woman earlier. I was looking up at him, hopefully, and we were smiling stupidly at each other. "I don't actually speak Spanish," he said, his lips forming the words but my own voice coming out of them.

I exhaled, and with it tears ran from the outer creases of my closed eyes to my ears and down into my hair, splayed out on the towel. It was easier for so long to nod and walk onward in silence pretending I understood. It was easier to make it up based on what I thought I heard. Now, as another wave crashed inside my chest, I knew I was wrong to think that for so long. And I cried some more before it was time to open my eyes again.

My husband and I managed to muddle through the rest of our vacation without a translator, even though we stared stupidly at each other a few times when we couldn't muster anything else. As time went on, we started to remember phrases from each other's language, relearning what we once thought was correct.

What emerged at the end of reintegration was some kind of beautiful Marriage Pig Latin: a colloquy that was not quite any language at all, sounded ridiculous to outsiders, and was understood clearly by its creators because, in the end, it was astoundingly, annoyingly simple.

Lori Volkman spent a career as an attorney and is the communications director for the Military Spouse JD Network. Now the owner of Trajectory Communications, she is a consultant for companies reaching out to military families. Her writing has appeared in *Readers Digest* and *The New York Times At War*. As a Navy brat and Navy wife, Lori has learned that homecoming is not the magic pill that cures deployment.

Moving the Lighthouse

Thomas Litchford

A rooster stood sentinel on a weather-beaten porch as my wife, Danielle, and I watched the sunrise over a deserted North Carolina beach. What stands out most prominently in my memory of that springtime visit to the Outer Banks was the sight of the Cape Hatteras Lighthouse. The tallest brick lighthouse in the country, it is probably what most people imagine when they hear the word "lighthouse," a slender white tower with a black stripe winding around it like the stripe on a peppermint stick.

We made the trip from our duty station at Norfolk, Virginia, to the Outer Banks, a string of barrier islands. Made mostly of sand, the islands are moving ever so slowly westward, gnawed by wind and waves from the east.

The first lighthouse on Hatteras was completed in 1803 to help ships avoid running aground on Diamond Shoals, a collection of sandbars in the treacherous waters near the cape, where the southbound Labrador Current meets the northbound Gulf Stream. A half-century later, the lighthouse was raised from 90 to 150 feet. By the 1860s, it had fallen into disrepair, and Congress ordered the construction of a new light. The new Cape Hatteras Lighthouse, lit in 1870, rose to nearly 200 feet from its foundation to its peak. It was built on a floating foundation of pine logs, giving it both flexibility and stability on the sandy island. Even that footing could not prevent the ocean from eating away at the shoreline, however.

In 1999, a massive crew of engineers and tradesmen moved the lighthouse 2,900 feet—over a half-mile—to a new location farther away from the encroaching Atlantic Ocean. The site of the first lighthouse is now underwater.

We visited Hatteras and the lighthouse right before Danielle's second deployment and my first PCS alone as a Navy spouse. When Danielle left, I would have to figure out how to pack up the life we had built over three and a half years in Norfolk and reassemble it in Newport, Rhode Island. Once Danielle detached from her ship and joined me in our new house, she would be teaching and working on a master's degree. I had no idea what I would be doing.

Up to that point in my life as a military husband, I'd had two kinds of jobs: The kind that didn't pay well but made for good stories and the kind that didn't pay well, but helped me sleep at night.

At the beginning of our first assignment at Newport, while Danielle attended Surface Warfare Officers School, I worked at a coffee shop called Java Bob's. Bob kept two plastic jars under the front counter labeled "Rent" and "Taxes." Into these he occasionally threw apparently random amounts of cash from the till.

Later I worked for another Bob, who managed an apartment complex in Newport. I once heard a tenant complaining she was being treated unfairly. Bob said, "That's not true. I hate you all equally." For most of our time in Norfolk, I worked for a small nonprofit that had been mismanaged for years and was teetering on the brink of bankruptcy. I preferred the nonprofit.

When Danielle and I were just a couple of hot young hipsters with no kids, we were not bothered by the way Danielle's career took precedence over mine. Our motto was "Anything But Boring," and the Navy helped us live by it. But not long after the boxes were unpacked in Newport the second time, the aimless trajectory of my career stopped being fun. It was no longer enough that I had amusing and offbeat stories to tell at the end of the day.

I had not been able to find work with a charitable organization like the one I'd left in Norfolk. In fact, I'd gone in the exact opposite direction and had taken a job at a car dealership. I worked with a Tony-Soprano-wannabe general manager; a slick, too-smart business manager; a misogynistic hard-living sales leader; a downtrodden middle-aged woman who was verbally abused by the rest of the sales team; and a defeated veteran who could sell some cars if he would only pick up the phone. Even this colorful cast of characters somehow failed to make up for the fact that I was working at an unfulfilling job. Danielle called it my Dark Period.

Naturally, it was time to have a baby.

We had been talking about this for a while. But the fact that I had no career to speak of made the decision easier. We would have a baby while Danielle was on a shore tour, and I would stay home as a full-time father. Some people thought the idea was unconventional. My pastor once asked me, "How will your children know you're a man?"

We don't go to that church anymore.

A near-stranger at a party told me he didn't think dads made very good moms. Most people thought it was awesome. The math was flawless: I had never earned more than a quarter of Danielle's income. If I continued working dead-end jobs, I might make just enough to pay for decent childcare, but I would still be working a dead-end job, so why work away from home at all?

I did find some meaningful work. One of the last deals I closed before the dealership folded was with a Navy chaplain who told me he didn't know of anyone writing from the point of view of the male military spouse. It was the spark of an idea. I emailed the editor of *Military Spouse* magazine and submitted a piece of writing. The editor didn't print that article, but she did ask for another one. Within a few months' time, I had the column I would write for the next five years.

When Danielle and I got married, my father read a wedding-ceremony favorite from the fourth chapter of Ecclesiastes, "Two are better than one … If either of them falls down, one can help the other up." (*NIV*)

I've often marveled at how any military service member gets by without a spouse. Who stays home with sick children? Who picks up the dry-cleaning? Who pays the bills?

When Danielle began her department-head tour on her last ship, it became much harder for us to support each other, to stay connected. She had the ship; I had our son, Sean, as a full-time occupation. She worked all day; I parented all day. When she came home, my patience with Sean was fully exhausted, and we would fight until bedtime.

I was on a short trip to Michigan, and Danielle was somewhere off the Horn of Africa when I got her email saying she needed to do something other than be a surface warfare officer. Thinking about life after the Navy was terrifying to me. The economy was still in recession, and I hadn't worked more than a few hours a month for the past five years. The risks inherent in such a big change were very real. Everything we'd built over a decade of marriage could collapse, but something had to give.

Before the Cape Hatteras Lighthouse was moved, storms would sometimes drive the ocean's waves up as high as the foundation of the lighthouse. The sands of Hatteras Island were shifting westward. The structure had to be moved or risk being swallowed by the sea.

When Danielle felt the waves lapping at her feet, she knew something drastic had to be done. Toward the end of her last deployment, she applied to a program that would allow her to serve as a military professor at the US Naval Academy. We waited for months and made contingency plans. We checked the web postings for the results from the selection board every day. Finally, we received word that Danielle's application had been approved. The selection board had named her among only five applicants chosen for the program. We moved to Annapolis, Maryland, a few months later, a slightly safer distance from the frothy Atlantic waters.

My role as a military spouse is to support my wife as she serves our country. I do what needs to be done. In a way, the military spouse's task is to be steadfast and portable. Be the strong, unwavering presence at home, but also be able to pack up and go wherever the mission requires you to go. But to say that a military spouse's role in life is to support a service member implies that the support flows only one way. This is not an accurate picture of most military marriages. A husband and wife must support each other or the marriage is doomed. Staying on solid ground requires a firm foundation and the ability to shift. Even if that means moving the lighthouse.

Thomas Litchford is a Navy husband, a father, and a freelance writer. His work has been featured in *Military Spouse* magazine and other publications. In his twelve years as a Navy spouse, he has learned to enjoy being the only guy at the table.

Smokin' Hot Romance

Jacey Eckhart

I didn't marry a smokin' hot guy in uniform so that I could toddle off to the commissary for American cheese and white bread. I wanted nights of unbridled longing. I wanted romance. I wanted to be swept away by passionate kissing, dammit.

I got that. Whoo, boy, I got that. And a lot more—including the American cheese and white bread, thanks.

The thing about a military romance is that it is so intense at the beginning that even the most practical woman—or man—throws all caution to the wind and agrees to follow this sailor, soldier, Marine, airman or Coastie to the ends of the earth. You don't really want that wicked romance to end, do you?

You do not want to go from passionate kisses to a dry little peck on the cheek worthy of Eleanor Roosevelt. You don't want to be the wife who gets so caught up in her kids that her husband develops a mom fixation worthy of Elvis. Most of all, you do not want to be that couple who drifts so far apart over the dishwasher and the deployments and the all-too-frequent moves that you can hardly remember why you went on this adventure in the first place.

Every time I hear about a break-up like that I have to take to my bed with a cup of green tea and a hot water bottle. Do those people think true love happens every day?

It doesn't. That is why I always pay attention to those older military couples who still like each other and enjoy each other's company. I pay attention to the ones who hold hands. I spy on the ones who can make each other laugh, because I want to learn their secrets.

Anyone can be in love the first year they meet, but it takes something else to still be in love ten or twenty or forty years later. How do those people deal with all those swim meets and spelling words and closets spilling forth with military gear without losing the romance?

They work at it. No, I take that back. "Work at it" sounds unpleasant. Like something you would do at a gym. Let's say instead that they organize their lives to maximize all the love they gather along the way. They tend the relationship. They make some room for talking and hugging and kissing and, well—sex. Here are a few things I've learned from still-in-love couples during my many years as a Navy wife and military columnist that might help keep every military romance simmering for years.

Kiss like you deploy tomorrow. Every civilian thinks that we military folks spend the weeks during deployment caught up in rapturous last-minute sex. Not so much. The weeks of preparation before deployment are a lot more like having your head waxed very, very slowly.

Because the days leading up to deployment are stressful, the deployment kisses have to happen every day. I don't mean you have to rush out to his car when he comes home and stick your tongue down his throat for half an hour. My on-base neighbor in Rhode

Island, when she heard her sailor's car roll up to the driveway, would go out to meet him, kiss him, tell him she was glad he was home. They would walk arm in arm up the driveway.

I stole that trick immediately and made it my very own. How easy is it to set the right tone for the evening with a kiss? That kiss is the signal to you to stop and realize that your service member won't always come home every night. He'll be in the field. She'll go on TDY. They will, in fact, deploy. So make the most of every homecoming by starting it with a kiss.

Find out what makes them happy—and do that. I once worked with a Marine sergeant major who claimed he divorced his first wife because she wouldn't send him a care package.

"There she was surrounded by Walmarts and Targets and Costcos and she couldn't be bothered to buy me socks," he exclaimed. He swore that was all the proof he needed to know that she didn't really love him.

That sergeant major scared the crap outta me. Because I rarely send my husband a care package when he's deployed. But here's the thing: My guy doesn't like care packages full of snacks because he is always trying to lose weight while he's on the ship. And he has plenty of socks.

I think the lesson I really learned from that sergeant major is to pay attention to what matters most to our partners. Find out what makes them feel loved and do it. My guy responds well to short suggestive emails. If he were happier to get socks, I would send him socks. Figure out what works and do that again and again. Save yourself some time and energy. Give him or her that thing they say they want most instead of all the stuff other people think they need.

In my unscientific opinion, a smokin' hot military romance includes a lot of sexy activity between two people who love each other. Figuring out the things you want and the things your partner wants is all part of the joy of being married. Apply yourselves.

Figure out what makes them mad—and don't do that. I once interviewed a Navy couple who married each other when they were eighteen. He had just graduated from boot camp. She was barely out of high school. Neither one of them knew jack about how to pay their phone bill much less how to keep a relationship alive. Yet twenty years later, he was a Navy master chief and she was a certified counselor. They were living their happily ever after with their three kids.

"I think our secret is that we figured out what made the other person mad and we stopped doing that," the wife said. "I don't think a lot of couples do that. I see them do the opposite." Me, too. What makes your partner mad that you could stop doing right now?

Keep your marriage at the center of the family. You will see lots of military families that seem to revolve around the kids, their needs, their activities, their presence. That ain't sexy. Having kids at the center of your marriage is a really good formula for being parents only instead of the hot lovers you want to be.

Keep your marriage as the center of your family. Be husband and wife all the time, then step out of those roles to be dad and mom to your kids on an as-needed basis. When your kids are little, "as needed" is pretty constant. You will both be parenting a lot. The goal is to get as many adult minutes together as possible.

Some couples do this by making their bedroom off limits to kids. Kids don't bring toys in the master bedroom. Kids don't enter without knocking. Kids sleep in their own rooms. Other couples have an adults-only date night. For us, what worked best when our kids were young was to keep a strict bedtime for the kids so there was time for us to reconnect at night. I especially needed that kid-free time to disconnect from my inner mommy and start feeling like myself again.

My military girlfriends and I noticed that when our kids were little, we wanted our bedrooms right next to theirs so we could hear them if they called in the night. Then the kids grew old enough to sleep through the night. Then they were old enough to get their own Cheerios and turn on *Sesame Street* by themselves without getting into any trouble. Then they were old enough to know what we were doing when we told them we were going to "take a nap." Uh oh. If your kids are old enough to have "Family Life" classes at school, take advantage of your next PCS to move your bedroom to a more private part of a new house.

Think of it this way: What will you do to signal to your kids that your marriage is the bedrock that the family is built upon?

Celebrate Naked Day. At least we call 'em Naked Days at our house. You can call them anything you like as long as you do not tell our moms or our kids that we are up to no good. Here's how it works: Every once in a while, ask your service member to take off one day, maybe during a not-as-crazy-as-usual time at work. Send the kids to school or daycare as usual. Then the two of you stay home. You don't go shopping. You don't run errands. You put the kids on the bus and then go back to bed to talk, laugh, and catch up on your … um … sleep.

In the military, our lives are on fast forward all the time. This is one way to make the world stop on a Tuesday—and the benefits can last all week.

Remember how you met—or almost didn't meet. Everyone has a how-we-met story. Maybe your soldier's workmate moved into your apartment building. Maybe you and your sailor served together on the same ship. Maybe your mom introduced you to this nice boy she worked with at the Pentagon. However you met, there are a million and one things that could have happened to prevent the two of you from ever laying eyes on one another.

Go ahead and imagine that. Tell the story to your kids. Ask other couples how they met, and tell them your story. True love is a little miracle in this world. Celebrate it.

Reconnect with high school. This is not an invitation to go stalk old boyfriends or girlfriends from high school on Facebook. (I do this, of course, but I don't want to talk to any of them. Mostly, I want to enjoy that dodged-a-bullet feeling.)

Instead, try to connect with your high school selves—those teenage people who had all the time in the world and nothing to do with it. Play songs that turned you on in high school. Drive around with the windows down and the stereo blasting. Go lie on a blanket together next to the nearest body of water. Dance around your kitchen and sing with a spatula for a microphone.

Your real self is not just the person who gets up and goes to work every day. Your service member is not just a person who wears a lot of polyester and unfashionable footwear. The two of you fell in love for a reason. Keep remembering what that reason was—and still is—now and forever.

Jacey Eckhart is the director of spouse and family programs for Military.com, a syndicated columnist, radio personality, and author of *The Homefront Club* (Naval Institute Press). She is also an Air Force brat, Army mom, and Navy wife, and is probably kissing her sailor in the driveway this very minute.

Locations: Yours, Mine, and Ours

Sarah Smiley

*W*hen my husband returned from a yearlong deployment overseas, he was, of course, sent on a new military assignment—in a different state. We found ourselves up against the modern military dilemma: Which spouse concedes to the other's career?

Back when I first became a military wife in 1999, that choice was easy. It was customary for people to urge new military brides to consider careers that could travel. Nursing and teaching were touted as especially military friendly because they are somewhat transportable. It was considered incompatible to be a lawyer or doctor and marry a man in the military. I mean, how could you work your way up in the practice or firm if you had to move all the time?

Today, however, women are gaining on men for the status of primary breadwinner. Women are holding more high-level positions in companies. Mobility is not their first career consideration. Their aspirations aren't easily put on hold or set aside. American culture has tipped from one that automatically casts women as the homemaker to one that views successful, career-oriented women as a given.

In contrast, the military lifestyle hasn't changed as much over the last generation. Service members still make relatively decent pay at a young age. They still look great in a uniform. And—here's the biggie—they still move every few years.

So far, the military hasn't changed the requirement for frequent moves. I suppose it can't. As my own military husband tells me, the military isn't in the business of making marriages.

As women make more money and have access to better jobs, they will be less able—and less willing—to follow a service member wherever military orders command. Whereas the uniform was once an asset for eligible bachelors, now it could be a deal breaker. And let's not forget: nothing aids service retention like a happy spouse.

So when this question came up on the eve of our latest PCS move, we wondered: Should I give up everything I've worked for and follow him? Or should he end a sixteen-year military career and stay with me?

The decision-making process was agonizing. There were no easy answers. Dustin is within years of retirement. After a decade of following him, I'm finally on my way to building my own career.

Eventually, we came to a compromise: We would live in both places. We'll maintain a house in one city, an apartment in the other, and we will commute back and forth. It isn't ideal, but it allows us both to pursue our goals without being resentful of the other.

We aren't alone. Many military families are making similar "geo-bachelor" arrangements. But these are short-term solutions. I can only agree to living in two cities at once for a single tour, not a whole career.

Luckily, because Dustin's retirement isn't too far off, our arrangement will be brief. There are plenty of young couples at the beginning of their careers who will meet these dilemmas with less room for compromise and more time to live it out.

Is the military ready to address this new, evolving face of marriage?

I doubt it.

The institution has proven resistant to change. Service members will move every two to three years for decades to come. But the culture and the world around the military, especially as it pertains to women and familial roles, will continue to transform.

Military marriages, it seems, will have to adapt on their own.

Sarah Smiley is a Navy wife, syndicated columnist, and author of several books, including *Dinner With the Smileys* (Hyperion). Sarah has been a Navy dependent since the day she was born, which should mean she knows everything and is super calm and well prepared. But she doesn't and isn't.

Speaking the Same Language

Jocelyn Green

*O*ur love story really isn't very different from yours. We met. We hit it off. In a very short time, we knew we would end up marrying each other. We had a very intentional courtship, because when one of you is in the military, you seriously don't have time to waste. Ten months later, we were married and— two days later— we were driving to Rob's next Coast Guard duty station in Homer, Alaska.

Then something happened during our first year of military marriage: ordinary, everyday life. And though we knew we loved each other, our methods of expressing that love were breaking down.

Here's what happened in our own words:

Jocelyn: I feel most loved when Rob and I spend quality time together, either doing things we enjoy or having quality conversations. So what do you do when your military spouse leaves on a ship for weeks or months at a time?

I thought I had a great idea. I bought a really nice leather-bound blank journal with the intention of trading it back and forth between us. I would write letters to Rob in the journal when I was home alone, which felt like spending quality time with him. When he returned, he could read it and know that I was thinking of him during his absence. That part went fine.

But when I gave the journal to him and asked him to do the same thing while he was a very busy Executive Officer on a Coast Guard cutter? Um … not so much.

Rob: When I was out at sea, I needed to be focused on my ship, the crew, and our mission. Out at sea—especially as XO—you're basically on duty around the clock. Having already spent two years on a cutter before I met Jocelyn, my idea of relaxing was vegging out to a movie in the wardroom—not writing in a journal.

Jocelyn: Clearly, my expectations for that journal were dramatically altered. If I could find it today, it would still be mostly blank.

But it wasn't only during separations that my craving for quality time affected our relationship. Every time Rob got home from being underway, I wanted to soak up time with him, just the two of us. So when he wanted to go hang out with friends right away after being at sea, I took it very personally. I felt hurt and unloved.

Rob: We had been assigned to a little town in Alaska, where I had already spent two years on a previous Coast Guard tour and had built up a great network of friends. I was looking forward to reconnecting with them, and at first it was a little frustrating that Jocelyn seemed to want to monopolize my home time. I didn't realize her need for quality time, and if I had, I definitely would have been more sensitive to it.

Jocelyn: Rob understands love best when it is expressed in acts of service. Oh, how I wish I had discovered this early on. I was fairly independent already, since I had already lived on my own before we were married. But I made the mistake of expecting Rob to do some of the same things my dad had done—even though Rob was gone much of the time. I let some things go and made a list of things for Rob to fix or do upon his return. My thought was, "He's the husband. He should do these things."

Rob: But my thought when I got back home after a few weeks out at sea was, "Oh great, I'm just a handyman now." And I'm not very handy! So after weeks and weeks of "XO, do this—XO, do that" from the ship's captain, I felt like I was in the same situation at home. I was already tired, so I would spend the first couple of days home in a sour mood. If she had taken care of those chores without me, I would have felt much more loved, but she didn't understand my love language.

Jocelyn: The moral of our story, of course, comes back to two principles: First, the things that make a wife feel loved may not be the same things that help her husband feel loved—and vice versa. Second, couples can learn to express love to each other in ways that each can understand and receive it. These days, Rob shows he loves me by spending quality time with me after the kids are in bed, by either having a conversation or watching Netflix together. Likewise, because I know it makes Rob feel loved, I make a concerted effort to have dinner on the table when he gets home from work, and to take care of as much household and car maintenance as I can on my own.

We learned that the first step in decoding tension in a marriage is discovering which expressions of love speak most clearly to each other. Without taking the time to learn that, misunderstandings and resentment can easily grow. When couples know how to love each other effectively, a struggling marriage can gain traction again, and a good marriage can become great.

Jocelyn Green is the wife of a Coast Guard veteran and the award-winning author of several books, including *Faith Deployed* (Moody) and *The 5 Love Languages Military Edition: The Secret to Love That Lasts* (Northfield) with Gary Chapman. Jocelyn says the biggest prize in her writing career was learning to apply the love languages to her own marriage.

Love's Tide Stronger Flows

Chris Stricklin

*A*t my first operational duty assignment, I worked closely with a captain who insisted that the Air Force had cost him his marriage. In the nineteen years since, I continued to hear from other military members about marital problems caused by military life.

When my wife and I marked our twentieth wedding anniversary, I was in Kabul, Afghanistan. From 8,000 miles away, I began reflecting on what the military had done to our marriage and our lives. In good times and bad, the military has been the catalyst to our relationship development. Though it has not been without painful and difficult times, much of what the military has done to my marriage has helped make it stronger.

The situations we experience in military life may be out of our control, but our reactions are not. Here are some of the ways my wife and I choose to approach our marriage and the demands of military life:

Marriage is not a two-way street. If it were, then each spouse would be going in a different direction when they should be on a one-way adventure together. Military life is filled with twists, turns, and detours, never a straight road. We found that instead of reciprocating with each other, we must walk hand-in-hand in the same direction. For any major choice driving a significant change in our future, we discuss our wishes and determine our next step.

Marriage is not a fifty-fifty proposition. It is not a math equation. Success requires that both partners give one hundred percent. Early in our marriage, I thought everything in the relationship should be fifty-fifty. But this mentality only encourages scorekeeping. If I devote my life to one person until death, do I really want to go halfway? Through moves, assignments, training, and deployments, military life has developed in us a determination to be all in. Whether it was loading household goods on a moving truck, unpacking that last box of the move, dragging the kids from school to school, or all the daily challenges of raising a family in a military setting—regardless of the challenge before us, we held hands and jumped in together each time.

Random acts of flowers. The real reason I discovered this principle is because the Air Force sends me TDY about every year on my wife's birthday and most Valentine's Days, so on random days I stop on my way home from work and bring her flowers. I use a blank card and write an original message. I found these flowers mean more to my wife than flowers dictated by official holidays. A few years back, during a move, her jewelry box fell open when we were packing, and I discovered she had kept all the little love notes from the random flowers I had given her over the years.

Fight elegantly. In the beginning of a marriage, a couple must learn not only how to live together, but how to fight constructively. When we argue, we stick to the issue and do not resort to insults and past issues. Because of the high-stress, high-risk environment of military life, we decided early on we had to resolve fights before going to sleep. This way, we wake every day in love and never run the risk of having our last words be heated ones.

Love's tide stronger flows. The Roman poet Sextus Propertius proclaimed, "Always toward absent lovers love's tide stronger flows." Although I hate being stationed away from my family, I get more quality talks with them when I am thousands of miles away than most families do sitting on the same couch. When you sit down in your living room after work, someone is doing homework and texting, someone is getting a snack in the kitchen, and most families are watching television. During deployment, I have screen time with my wife first thing in the morning and last thing before bed. We have to be intentional about our communication and align our schedules. Because we are staring at a computer or phone screen to talk to each other, our attention is not sidetracked with TV or other distractions. The conversation has our undivided attention. Being apart actually brings us closer together.

The honeymoon is never over. Time apart is a challenge for military couples, but the reunions are amazing. Every time we reunite it feels like our honeymoon all over again, like the feeling of holding hands after our wedding. The extreme closeness of actually being together. Staring into each other's eyes again. Leaning across the table and stealing a kiss in public. That is a feeling you can't buy, you can't manufacture, and you can't fake. We get that feeling often, because we don't know how long a stolen moment will last before the Air Force separates us again.

Say "I love you" often. I appreciate my wife more than she will ever know. I try to earn her love every day. Our teenagers tease us saying, "You guys are not teenagers in love!" What bigger compliment could they pay us?

Chris Stricklin has been married to his high school sweetheart for twenty years and is the father of four. When he is not committing random acts of flowers, Chris spends his time flying fighter jets for the Air Force.

Eat It.
It's Good for You!

Military Parenting

··· ~ ···

"All you need is love.
But a little chocolate now and then doesn't hurt."
~ Charles M. Schulz

Strength of a Little Warrior

Jacqueline Goodrich

*T*he morning I picked up the phone and heard the dreaded words, "I'm calling from Afghanistan to inform you that your husband … " I was lying in bed with our eleven-day-old son, Tag. My mom was downstairs, playing with our daughter, Lucy, so they missed seeing me melt down and hearing me cry, "Oh my God! Is he okay?" repeatedly into the phone.

When I pulled myself together enough to tell Lucy the news, I didn't know the full extent of Michael's wounds or how bad things would get. The week between being notified and being able to meet him at his hospital bed was emotionally charged. Lucy, at three years old, picked up on the anxiety and broke down in my arms, sobbing.

"I'm so sad about Daddy's boo boos, Mommy."

She desperately wanted to see his face and know that he was safe. Before the events of that week, all Lucy understood about deployment was that we miss Daddy when he is gone. Now, the real truth was out. When he is away, we also fear for his life.

Before arriving at Walter Reed National Military Medical Center, I was told that it would help if I saw Michael before Lucy did. That way I could experience my own emotional process and then be able to help her through the daunting task of approaching her wounded super hero. I was nervous and shaking when I first saw him, but when Lucy saw him, all she saw was her daddy. Beneath the tubes, bandages, IVs, and scratches, she recognized a warrior. My heart soared when she climbed up into bed with him and starting kissing his head.

The first time Michael was released from the hospital to spend a weekend at home may have been more stressful than the week of his injury. Caring for Tag was natural for me, but caring for Michael with Lucy scared me. Lucy was so excited to have Daddy back, I was afraid she would hurt him accidentally. I knew if she did, she would feel horrible, and it would make it harder for them to connect. Michael was able to walk, but only with a cane, and even that was slow and unsteady. I watched in awe as Lucy helped him. She held his free hand while his other hand had a death grip on his cane. An eighty-year-old could have walked circles around Michael, but Lucy stayed perfectly in step with him. I never once had to tell her to slow down. She was patient beyond her three years. Any time Michael got up, I was a ball of nerves, fearful he would fall. The way Lucy looked at him was totally different. She was confident. She knew his limitations and that he was still badly hurt, but she also sensed his potential for healing.

Our stay at Walter Reed was not as brief as the "couple of weeks" we were initially told. We were there for five months, and that took a toll on Lucy. We soon noticed that spending more than five or six days in a row at the military hospital made her sad and anxious. My parents lived just two hours away, so we were able to let her go home with them every other week, while I stayed at the Fisher House to be near Michael. The downside to this arrangement was that Lucy worried about us when she was with her grandparents, and then felt guilty for missing home when she was with us at the Fisher House.

Her days at the hospital exposed her to things that few children her age experience. The effects of war in her life included an endless line of doctors for her daddy, recovery contraptions, and prosthetics. Though Michael's leg was saved, Lucy still learned all about the prosthetics that many of our friends wore. That's not something I'd planned to teach my children about before kindergarten. For Lucy and Tag, it became commonplace. Lucy can explain to anyone what prosthetics are and how they work. One day after appointments, we were walking from the hospital to the Fisher House, and she spotted a woman on a bicycle. She started jumping up and down with excitement and said, "Mommy! Daddy! Look! It's a girl warrior! She has a new leg, and she can ride a bike now!" This level of little-girl admiration and wonder is usually reserved for ballerinas or Disney princesses. Not for Lucy.

Michael and I never expected our children to have their innocence interrupted or for their character to be developed this way. Because Lucy has lived among the wounded, she understands more than most children what bravery costs. Through our time at Walter Reed, the kids and I witnessed new life rising up from the ashes of combat as we watched grown men and women learning to walk and live again.

When we moved home, Michael still had a couple of years of recovery to go, but we were hopeful that Lucy would be able to heal emotionally at home. The therapists who met with us at Walter

Reed were amazed that Lucy was always very open and willing to talk to us about her feelings. That continued after we went home, and sometimes it was downright painful for us, as parents. The numbness we all felt at the early stages of our journey wore off. As Lucy grew, she was able to verbalize more feelings and questions. Sometimes the questions were simple to answer on her level, but it was still heartbreaking to have to explain to her the extent of hatred that exists in this world.

"Mommy, what was in that rocket that hit Daddy?"

"Why would someone make a rocket?"

"Do people watch war? Like in baseball seats, Mommy?"

"Did they watch Daddy get hurt? Is it a game to them?"

"Did they capture Daddy?"

"Are there bad guys in heaven?"

"Why do they have so much hate inside them?"

Many answers left her in tears. Some of her questions simply have no answers. As an adult with a soul and a beating heart, I don't understand the kind of hatred that wages war on military and civilians alike. It's something I do not want to think about, but Lucy is brave enough to ask the tough questions. Her heart is as fiercely loyal and patriotic as her daddy's.

As time passed, I became more nervous about how Lucy would feel about her daddy returning to the Army, even if on a reserve status. Would her anxiety get worse? How could she possibly understand why we would still want to continue serving as an Army family?

The answer to my questions came when her little ears overheard a conversation. I used the phrase "new job" as we discussed what full-time career Michael would pursue after his recovery. We didn't know she was listening, but she chimed in, clearly upset.

"No! Daddy can't get a new job!" She cried out.

We were shocked by her outburst, and I wanted her to be very clear and certain about her feelings. I asked if she understood that Daddy staying in the Army, active duty or not, would mean he could go back to war again. He could get hurt again. Worse could happen. I asked her if she understood.

My proudest moment as the parent of this little warrior was when she stuck out her chin with intense pride and simply said, "Yes. My daddy has to stay in the Army. Because my daddy is a warrior."

Jacqueline Goodrich is an advocate for families, particularly children, of wounded warriors through the nonprofit she founded, The General's Kids. She is the dedicated wife of a soldier and the mother of two beautiful children.

Our Hearts Are Big Enough

Julia Gibbs

*T*he chaos and excitement of the grand arrival at the airport had died down, and we were finally at home as a family of five, exhausted but exuberant. Our seven-year-old daughter, Mattox, sat beside me as I held her new baby brother in my arms. She looked distraught. I questioned her gently, assuming that she was simply overwhelmed by the newness of adding an adopted brother to the family.

"Mommy, he is so, so big!" She said a little sadly.

I was befuddled.

"Yes, he is very big for a thirteen-month-old baby," I said.

She let go of her new brother's chubby hand and looked at her own tiny hand.

"But we are so small, Mommy," she said.

I didn't understand where this conversation was going. Then she looked up at me and said, "That is how people are going to know he is adopted, 'cause he is so big and we are small!"

Bless her. We are the color of milk and our sweet Moses is the color of dark molasses, but Mattox never saw that. She just worried that people would notice he was larger than the rest of the family.

Our desire to adopt started early in life, but was solidified while we were stationed in Korea. My aviator husband flew long days and even longer nights during that year, and I quickly discovered that I was not made to watch paint dry on the inside of our apartment.

I didn't have a job nor any children at the time, so when a friend asked me to help her out at a local orphanage, I jumped at the opportunity. It was there, working with those children who had no mommy to rock them to sleep and no daddy to tickle their bellies, that the call to adopt became a mission for our family. Four assignments, four years, two biological children, and one deployment later, we were ready to start our paperwork to adopt when we got orders to Stuttgart, Germany.

While living overseas, I began with the tools I had at hand, online and by phone. I researched agencies, countries, and social workers. Our initial thought was to adopt from the United States through the foster care system. That idea quickly hit a brick wall. We were told that living in a foreign country made us ineligible to adopt from most programs in the United States. Agency after agency gave me the same answer: No.

No: They would not work with a military family who was living abroad.

No: A military family is much too unstable for an adoptive child.

No: An adoption would take years to complete, and with our moving schedule it would be impossible.

No, no, no! I might have done a little frustrated screaming in the back yard, but nothing too extreme for my reserved German neighbors.

Then the breakthrough came. I finally discovered that a military family, while stationed overseas, is not considered "international," because a US military installation by law is considered part of the United States. For legal adoption purposes, we were on US soil while connected to a military base or post. Still, some agencies were hesitant about our case.

I finally found an agency in Colorado willing to work with us. We were their first military family, so I took on the challenge of blazing a new trail for other families like ours, while also trudging through the trenches of an international adoption from the Democratic Republic of Congo.

The paperwork tried to drown us; the red tape was determined to hold our heads under, but we kept treading water and stayed afloat. I knew that a baby was at the end of the journey, and that assurance fueled my every step. We had to call the American embassy in Frankfurt numerous times, email the embassy in Rome, and then the one in Kinshasa, DRC, several more times, but it was worth it. One February morning we received an email. It read, "Meet your son."

My heart stopped. I couldn't swallow. I felt the tears rushing unhindered from my eyes before I even opened his picture. And then, he was there. Our son. Our sweet Moses sat in front of a one-room shack on the jungle floor with a chicken posing casually beside him. I touched the screen and let my fingers trace his brown cheeks and distant eyes. He was ours, and I would do anything it took to bring him home.

For nine more long months, we worked from Germany with the United States government, the Congolese government, the German government, and our excellent support team in the office of the judge advocate general on post. I really should have had a bed in that office, because I spent days there reviewing documents, signing documents, and having them notarized.

When our time in Germany was done, we moved to Fort Rucker, Alabama, still without our son. Then three weeks after the boxes were unpacked, we got another email. It said, "Time to go get him."

My husband could not get permission to travel to a war-torn country, one which our government was actively warning citizens not to enter. So my dad, an old soldier, packed up to go with me on the thirty-five-hour trip across the world to get his grandson.

I can't exactly explain what it is like. The months of roller-coaster, hopes-up, hopes-dashed waiting. The myriad spontaneous breakdowns at a stoplight. The episodes of crying in the shower. The hours of agonized prayer on my knees. Then the anxious entry into an unstable country. The chaotic, nerve-wracking car ride to the orphanage. Always waiting for that moment.

Waiting for the moment I would walk through the door. The moment I would finally touch those sweet round cheeks that were permanently burned into my memory from an image on a computer screen. There are no real words for that moment. It's just too big, too overwhelming.

But then, it was suddenly here. My chubby Moses crawled through the door of the orphanage and into my arms. He sat and stared at my face. He touched my hair, and I touched his. He was afraid, and he didn't know me, but I knew him. I had prayed for this child, begged for this child, and loved this child from afar.

He sits beside me now, almost two years later, coloring as I type. He chases the dog, wrestles with his brother, sings with his sister, and laughs with his toothy grin.

He calls me, "Mama," reaching with greedy hands that love to be held. I call him "Mine," with a heart that might be small by my daughter's assessment, but is big enough to love the boy we call "Big Moe." And maybe that will be how others know that we have adopted him. Not the size of our stature, but by the size of our hearts.

A little family with big hearts.

Julia Gibbs is an Army wife, Army daughter, musician, and freelance writer. Her work has appeared in several newspapers, and she is working on her first novel. In her Army lifetime, Julia has moved more than nineteen times to three countries and seven states, collecting a soldier husband, three children, and a dog along the way.

Ready-Made Family

Sarah Holtzmann

My husband, Pat, is the total package. He is great at cooking and cleaning. He's responsible and caring. When I married him, I got another package deal: his three children from a previous marriage. Some people might call this a ready-made family, but there is no such thing. It takes work to make a family of any kind. Blending a family takes a lot of time, patience, and understanding from everyone concerned.

I wasn't totally prepared for all that this package deal included: the drama, conflict, and heartbreak that comes with creating one family from two. I wouldn't change my three stepchildren for the world; what I would change is all the pain they've had to endure to get to where we are today as a blended military family.

One of my husband's four long deployments was particularly stressful. He was fighting a war in Bagram, Afghanistan. I was teaching full-time, taking take care of a house by myself in the middle of winter in North Dakota, caring for my stepkids, and negotiating—sometimes unsuccessfully—with their mother. Neither she nor the children seemed to understand why Pat had to be gone. The kids just couldn't wrap their heads around war and separation, and they didn't know how to deal with it all. Like many moms during deployment, I felt like a metaphorical punching bag for everyone's frustrations.

Not only was I trying to help the kids deal with their father being deployed, I was also trying to fill their father's shoes to some extent, when he could not be there for regular days or special days, for ball games and birthday parties. At the same time, I was trying to take care of myself. I missed my husband desperately and worried about his safety.

I leaned on my own mother for basic deployment-related worries and stresses. My dad served in Vietnam, and my mom dealt with many of the same issues that military spouses deal with today: troubling news coverage of the war, not hearing from a spouse for long periods of time, people constantly questioning the safety of a deployed loved one.

While my mom knew the military spouse ropes, my husband's stepmother, Pam, knew about stepparenting. The stories she told about her own stepparenting experiences guided me through mine and gave me courage. She believed in me, which made me believe in myself. She inspired me to make stand up for myself and gave me hope that life could and should be better.

I did my best to work with the children's mother so I could spend quality time and build a relationship with the kids in their father's absence. Shared custody meant their lives were divided between two homes. I tried to prepare the kids for the regular transitions from one place to the other, planning ahead for everything from homework reminders to wardrobe needs and sleepovers with friends. When two households are concerned, advance preparation often must bend to changing schedules, so I stayed flexible whenever possible on drop-off and pick-up times.

Family matters are not games—especially during a deployment—and children should never be treated as pawns in a power struggle between divorced parents and stepparents.

During the emotional times—deployments, moving, the drama of custody disputes, the marriage of one of the children and all that goes with that milestone, grief over losing family members—I focused on the good times and leaned on family and friends.

Our blended family took a lot of work. Expanding our family wasn't easy either. After a struggle with infertility, we successfully conceived twins through in vitro fertilization. I was on modified bed rest for half my pregnancy. During that time, our older kids were amazing at helping out my husband around the house and driving me to medical appointments when needed.

That Christmas, my husband and I wanted to create a special holiday for them. We decorated the tree and opened presents on Christmas morning. We had planned a huge meal, but before it was ready to be served, my water broke. The twins were not due until February, but babies have minds and schedules of their own.

"Are you sure it broke?" asked my husband, who had slaved over the stove all day preparing the holiday feast.

"Yes, dear, we have to go."

The kids were troopers and headed over to friends' homes while we headed to the hospital. I hated that we missed out on Christmas Day with the family, but was excited for the arrival of our twins. Apparently, the twins did not want to miss out on Christmas with their new family either.

This Christmas experience embodies our journey. Events do not always turn out as planned; sometimes they turn out even better. Our journey of building a family was definitely not the way I once envisioned it, but I would do it all over again, in a heartbeat: loving my husband, caring for my stepchildren, gaining wisdom from my mom and his stepmother, and giving birth to our beautiful twins.

So here we are with our pureed family—we're way beyond blended—twin toddlers, two teenagers, an adult son and daughter-in-law, plus three grandchildren. As a mother, stepmother, grandmother, and wife, I am truly blessed.

Yes, it's sometimes a struggle. On most days, there's some name-calling going on in our household, but not usually the bad kind. I am called many names: Mama, Nana, Sarah, and sometimes Honey. My stepkids call me Sarah, and I love that. It makes me feel closer to them. I don't expect them to call me "Mom," because they have a mom. They also have a dad and a stepmom, brothers, and sisters. They are part of a strong military family—not one that was ready-made, but one that was created with determination, patience, and love.

Sarah Holtzmann is an Air Force daughter, Air Force wife, mother of two, stepmother of three, and grandmother of three. She taught kindergarten and second grade before becoming a stay-at-home mom. Sarah describes herself as the mother of many children, a teacher of many students, and a student of many mothers.

School Choices and Changes

Amanda Trimillos

School experiences for my military kids are different from the school days I knew as a child. My oldest has lived in four different states and attended three different schools in fewer than six years. My four-year-old twins have already lived in three states; my youngest is two-for-two. My greatest challenge after a move isn't finding a new house, church, or friends; it is settling into a new school. This is a driving factor in where we choose to live and worship, and the friends who become part of our family circle.

I am a military parent, but I also have experience as a middle and high school teacher. At every school and every base, I hear the same phrase from military families: "I wish I'd known that before we moved!" I try to help avoid that statement by asking leading questions: "I hear you just moved here. Do you have kids in school? How has the move affected them?"

I wait for their story, and I share.

Receiving orders to move initiates the first challenge for my family. Well-intentioned experts say parents must research and be aware of all there is to know about a new location before the move. But research is not as straightforward as they make it sound. Each base and locale presents a new set of challenges and priorities. In Altus, Oklahoma, I found little choice: five elementary schools, two middle schools and one high school. On the other extreme, my husband's assignment to the Pentagon kept me up at night with its plethora of choices. Fairfax County, Virginia, among the largest school districts in America, is home to more than a hundred elementary schools that feed into dozens of high schools. These options only scratched the surface of the number of school and district choices available between Maryland, the District of Columbia, and Virginia. Limited time before a move makes it impossible to investigate hundreds of schools to make an educated decision about where to live.

Moving across state lines causes frustration from the start, beginning with kindergarten. Our twin preschoolers missed the age cut-off in our current district, meaning they will start kindergarten just before they turn six. In other states, the age-cut off is later in the year, so at their next school, they could be significantly older than their classmates.

Differences in school calendars and requirements also pose a problem for mobile students. Families moving to schools whose semester is already underway find their children miss full units of learning. Or the reverse may be true, where a child is expected to repeat completed lessons and courses. Location-specific courses like state history classes are another source of repetition. A student may take state history in New Jersey and then again in Virginia, and then again in Alaska. The mandate for state history was met in their first location, but students who move might be expected to repeat the course requirement for each new state.

State standardized testing can also snarl moving plans. Our

neighbors in Virginia received orders for a May time-frame move to Georgia. Their transition meshed with the school schedule until course finals were postponed by fourteen snow days in Virginia. Missing one test at the end of the year could cause their daughter, a high school junior, to not get credit for the entire course. The family was faced with difficult choices. To avoid having the student retake the whole course at her new school in Georgia, the family could remain behind while the military member reported to the new unit, or their daughter could take the test early, covering material she hadn't yet learned.

Relocations can also challenge participation in extra-curricular activities. Students miss try-outs or become ineligible for teams simply based on military connection. Some students are denied lead positions in sports, drama, and student council. A coach told the daughter of one of my friends that she would not make the team because her parents were scheduled to move in two years. The coach refused to take a team spot away from a local student.

Fortunately, military families don't face these challenges alone or unrecognized. Most states have joined the Interstate Compact on Educational Opportunities for Military Children to support and protect military-connected children of active duty military, guard, reserve, and recruiting families during deployments and relocations. The compact actively works to encourage the remaining states to join and support military-connected families transitioning across their borders.

For the high school students I teach, accommodation for graduation stipulations are the most valuable aspect of the compact. When I taught at a Department of Defense Educational Activity school in England, I had several students who lived with friends to complete high school while their families moved stateside per military orders. I learned this was because of the difficulty of transferring credits in their junior and senior years from Department of Defense schools to stateside schools. Had they moved with their military parents, they would not be eligible for graduation nor for their awarded college scholarships, because all their completed courses would not transfer.

The interstate compact doesn't eliminate all issues, but now there are provisions that help facilitate graduation for students who move in their junior or senior year. The compact allows for waiving courses required for graduation if similar course work has been completed and flexibility regarding exit or end-of-course exams.

The interstate compact also encourages more support for students during a parent's deployment, allowing additional excused absences to alleviate deployment and reintegration challenges. Students must complete missed work, but the compact allows them to participate in deployment and reintegration activities from one month before deployment through six months after a parent returns.

Military parents are the best advocates for their children. Administrators are not often familiar with the compact for military-connected students or its guidelines and implications. Parents can get help from school liaison officers. These are civilians assigned to military installations, specifically to provide information for schools and a voice and support for military students and families, whether inbound or outbound.

As soon as a family has orders to move, a call to a student liaison officer can help with research and action in support of a child's education. The family who was stymied by snow days in Virginia reached out to their school liaison. As a result, school counselors in Georgia designed a plan for the incoming student, allowing the family to move together.

Parents can do many things to help their military-connected child thrive in school. No matter the student's age, parents should communicate with educators. The more a teacher knows about the situation at home, the better a teacher can plan supportive activities and lessons. As a parent, I take initiative to ask questions and offer ideas about how the school can support my own kids. I contact teachers, school counselors, principals, and parent teacher groups. I ask about clubs and evening events.

When we moved to New Jersey, my daughter knew only one route at her new school, from her classroom to the cafeteria and back. In week two, we cried together after school one day because she got lost trying to return books to the library. The next week she knew she would need to make her way to the main office. With my prompting, her teacher assigned her a walking buddy, who later became her best friend. Now I know to request school buddies for my children ahead of time. As a high school teacher, I see new students on a daily basis who are lost and don't want to ask for help. A designated buddy system allows even older students to make connections and navigate unfamiliar hallways. When we moved to Virginia, I was introduced to a parent buddy, part of a PTA strategy for helping whole families integrate into the school community. I now plan to ask for my own buddy at every new location, whether there is a formal system or not.

I also work to gently encourage classroom teachers and the school to support both military-connected students and their peers. When my husband deployed, my daughter's teacher suggested she create a memory book in class as a surprise Christmas gift. Not only was it fun for my daughter, it proved a wonderful connection across the globe and between family and teacher. The teacher surprised my daughter with having my husband read a book via video to her classroom.

No matter our efforts, military-connected students will have added challenges caused by relocations and deployments. These students will also have great adventures and exposure to a world not known to their peers. As parents, we can advocate for our kids and help them manage the challenges. We can highlight and encourage the adventure of growing up with the military. Perhaps with good information and advocacy, military children will be able to say, "I had a great adventure," and their parents will never have to say, "I wish I'd known that before we moved!"

Amanda Trimillos is a National Board Certified teacher and course leader at National University. She advocates for military-connected students and educators through the White House's Joining Forces: Operation Educate the Educator initiative. An Air Force wife, Amanda learned through eighteen years, seven moves, five deployments, and four kids that balancing the challenges and adventures depends on the perspective of parents and teachers together.

Home, Sweet Homeschool

Benita Koeman

*S*ix years ago, I embarked on an adventure that would cause me to feel full of insecurity and self-doubt, an adventure that would give me plenty of reasons to phone a friend for encouragement. Six years ago, I learned the meaning of curriculum and ordered one. My kitchen table was littered with books and projects—that part hasn't changed. Six years ago, I struggled to figure out how to work through fourth and second grade material simultaneously for my two sons, while my five-year-old daughter taught herself how to read. Six years ago, I began homeschooling my children.

I was always curious about the idea of homeschooling, and six years ago the Army gave me a good reason to try it. My husband received a six-month assignment to Fort Jackson, South Carolina. Apprehensive about putting our children in a new school for less than a whole school year, it was the nudge I needed to become a homeschool military mom.

A number of my homeschooling friends agree that a major challenge—shall we say, adjustment—to homeschooling is being with our kids all the time. We've discovered how wonderful it is to really get to know our kids because of the time we spend together. We've also witnessed the benefits to our children of having teachers who know them better than anyone, who can tailor their teaching to each child's individual needs and interests.

Homeschool parents feel the weight of their responsibilities acutely. We are always asking ourselves: "Am I doing enough? Are they learning enough? Are we missing anything that will affect their options down the road?" We work hard to be sure we are using good material and that our children are progressing as they should. Finding the homeschool program type—online, classical, traditional, video—and format —workbooks, instructional, textbooks—that works for each student is daunting. One of my friends commented that it is like being teacher and guidance counselor rolled into one. That's a lot of responsibility.

A great benefit of homeschooling is the flexibility it offers. There is flexibility to adjust to challenges with curriculum, schedule changes, and life changes as needed. Kids have the opportunity to learn at their own speed and in their own learning style.

Homeschool also offers freedom in scheduling, which is particularly helpful for a military family. When Dad is home from deployment or home on R&R, we can take time off from school and enjoy being reunited as a family. When Dad is off duty, so are we. When it's time to move, school is on pause for a time, unless the cross-country move turns into an educational field trip. Our time together strengthens family bonds and makes moving transitions a little easier at a new duty station when we're in that awkward phase of not knowing anyone.

Academic continuity is another homeschool plus for military families, because there's really nothing permanent about a permanent change of station. We don't have educational gaps caused by our children learning different concepts in different progressions in different schools. Our high schoolers don't have to worry about credits transferring from school to school. We can build a transcript based on our choices, not on what might or might not be available or required at a current or future assignment.

In each new neighborhood, it's exciting to find opportunities for extracurricular educational opportunities. While we were stationed in Hawaii, our boys learned how to surf and scuba dive, and they took sailing lessons at Pearl Harbor. We learned about the Hawaiian culture by visiting museums and attending local cultural events. We studied up on the events of the Pearl Harbor attack and toured the Battleship Missouri Memorial and USS Arizona Memorial. With the ocean so easily accessible, we were immersed in learning about the ocean with all of our senses. You can't capture that type of learning in a book or video. With homeschool, there is no homework or busy work, so pencil-and-paper class time is shorter, leaving more time open for field trips.

There are challenges specific to military homeschool families. Big ones. Homeschooling can be a full-time occupation. Depending on the age of the children, it may be difficult (but not impossible) for a homeschool parent to participate in outside activities or have a career. Taking advantage of work-at-home options or partnering with other homeschool parents offers flexibility here, too.

Homeschooling through deployment is especially challenging, because there is no break for the parent at home. Being part of a homeschool group can help. Other parents can trade babysitting or teaching duties to offer personal time to recharge.

Learning and implementing homeschool requirements for multiple locations is another challenge. Regulations vary from state to state and country to country. The Home School Legal Defense Association lists the homeschool requirements for each state or country and provides legal advice and other resources for members. Homeschool groups can also offer valuable information and real examples of what they have turned in to their particular state to fulfill requirements.

Homeschooling is a big decision. A family must weigh the options and decide whether it is the best choice for them. It might not be forever. It might be the answer to the challenges at a particular assignment or for a particular child, for a season or for a school career. There will be good days and bad ones, tough choices and shining rewards. Since our initial decision, our family has homeschooled through three moves and one deployment. With each move, we consider the best choice for our kids, and it continues to be schooling at home.

Benita Koeman is an Army wife and the creator of Operation We Are Here, a clearinghouse for military family resources and information. For the past six years, through three moves and one deployment, homeschooling has been the best, but not the easiest, option for Benita's family.

My Son's Battle

Judy Davis

W hen my husband chose to return to military service
after being a civilian for nineteen years, I had no
idea how it would impact our family of four from
the Midwest. I had never been in the military, I had never seen
a military installation, and I didn't know a single military brat.
In fact, my only connections to military life were the stories my
husband sometimes told about his earlier Army years, and the
information provided to me by cable news or breaking stories that
interrupted my favorite sitcom.

But there I was in the middle of my life, downsizing and
packing our family's belongings to support my husband's dream to
go back into the Army. In a matter of weeks, we were headed to our
first duty station. Green is the word that comes to mind—in both
experience and new Army wardrobe.

I had no idea what the impact of this transition would be on
our family or our teenage children. It was five years later when I
fully grasped the reality of military life and the effects wartime
service can have on the families of those who serve.

That was the day I got a call from our son. It wasn't the typical
"I procrastinated on my paper and need help meeting the deadline"
call that my friends were getting from their college-aged children.

This was the kind of call that brings you to your knees in an instant: "Mom, I'm not okay, and I need help."

On the other end of the line was a voice foreign to me, a voice of a young man who sounded like he had given up on life. In fact, if it hadn't been for the actions and support of his friends, my son might have taken his own life. My ray of hope in that moment was that he called me, he reached out for help.

Miles away from my son, with my husband about to leave for a pre-deployment training, I felt helpless and scared. Nothing prepared me for the hours and days that followed. How did we get to this place? How was it possible that at a time when my child needed me most, I was nowhere near him? It was possible because we are a military family and the likelihood of living near one another decreases with each new set of orders.

Our son was a typical healthy nineteen-year-old college student, or so we thought. He had friends, enjoyed his classes at Texas Tech University, and seemed to be adjusting well to life in Lubbock. It seemed that our transition to military life, even with my husband's deployment and all the upheaval that our move had caused, had little effect on him. Until reality came rushing in.

Our son's diagnosis was anxiety, mild depression, and severe post-traumatic stress disorder. It turns out our son had turned to prescription medications and alcohol as a way to drown out the feelings that had consumed his life since becoming a military dependent. I blamed and resented the Army for the fact that my baby had almost become a statistic. Then my husband deployed, and I was left to deal with this crisis without my better half by my side.

I didn't understand how my son could have PTSD. Everything I had learned from our last deployment briefing about this condition and how to recognize the signs came flooding back into my thoughts. I racked my brain, opened up to my battle buddies, and tried to connect that information to his behavior, but my son hadn't displayed any of the typical signs. He wasn't in the military, and he had never seen combat. My husband also had a hard time accepting this diagnosis. It tore me apart. How and why did this happen? As parents, we needed answers that no one could provide.

For weeks, I educated myself on all things post-traumatic stress. I learned that PTSD strips its victims of all hope, often leading to depression and addiction. Only later, after reaching out and seeking professional support, was I able to accept that, for my son, our life in the military and the residual effects of war were as devastating to him as they were for any combat veteran.

Like many other military dependents, my son gleaned from military culture that a military kid has to "soldier on." He witnessed teens step into a deployed parent's role and watched kids worry when their at-home parent had a rough day.

Finding an escape from the anxiety and worry was my son's way of dealing with military life. I regret that I didn't probe and question more. I wish I had realized, before my son became suicidal, that his abrupt change in behavior was actually an indication that something else was going on. But it was easier to dismiss what seemed to be typical teen moodiness rather than recognize it as the first sign of a more serious issue.

Instead, I saw what I needed to see—a healthy, helpful, resilient teen. I couldn't have been more wrong.

I look back now and see that I wasn't at all prepared to help my kids adjust to military life. My son almost paid the ultimate price because of it. I had no idea how this life would affect my children. I didn't realize that their needs, challenges, and struggles would be different than my own.

When I was learning the ropes of military life, sometimes my best was just keeping myself from falling apart. It was the reality of my life back then. But we learn, we grow, and we become stronger.

We got through this terrifying chapter of parenthood with lots of faith and support. We took comfort in support from family, battle buddies, professionals trained to help in situations like ours, and faith in a power greater than ourselves. Every step of the way, our support system pushed, encouraged, and called out bullshit as the need arose, never letting us wallow in the feelings of blame or guilt. They helped us focus on how far we have come. They reminded us that we couldn't prevent our son's choice to self-medicate, and that our parenting efforts provided lines of communication and understanding, allowing him to reach out to us at a crucial moment.

Depression and PTSD aren't conditions that our son will outgrow, nor something he must simply push through. Our son's condition is serious and requires treatment, As his family, we become part of that process. As our son continues to recover, I find peace and move forward by accepting things as they are and acknowledging that he is still with us today because we are standing with him, facing up to his struggle every day.

Judy Davis is an Army wife, motivational speaker, blogger, and author of *Right Side Up: Find Your Way When Military Life Turns You Upside Down* (Elva Resa). Judy became an advocate for healthy military life when she chose to share her family's experience with others. Together, she and her son cofounded Living Thru Crisis to help families and community leaders understand the unspoken truth about teen depression, suicide ideation, PTSD, and addiction.

Military Kids in a Civilian World

Randi S. Cairns

I was in the labor and delivery room, about to deliver our baby three weeks early. I spent the first hour of hard labor arranging childcare for my three other children and driving myself to the hospital. With the exception of the handful of medical professionals around me, I was alone. My Army National Guard husband was deployed.

I called the Red Cross right after I called my sister-in-law, and by the time my husband heard the news in Guantanamo Bay, I was red faced and pushing to the demands of trained strangers. Soon a cell phone was held to my left ear by a gloved hand. Across the static, my husband urged me, "Keep your legs closed and just wait." His flight home for mid-tour leave was a week away, but he was fairly sure he could get an earlier flight and wanted me to stall as long as I could.

It should be noted that keeping your legs closed does not, in fact, delay labor. My body's natural responses and the voices from the delivery room spoke with authority. Sara arrived less than an hour later. Her daddy arrived in time to hold her the next day, after miraculously catching a red-eye from Cuba during hurricane season.

We are a guard family living in a civilian setting. Many of my neighbors and hometown residents don't even know we're military.

We don't live in the idyllic town of my dreams where folks bring each other casseroles, where the older folks keep a watchful eye on the little ones on the street, or where a shared sense of community lends a sense of extended family.

As the date approached for Sara to be born, there was no offer to watch my children, drive me to the hospital, or hold my hand during labor. In the hospital, the arrival of my handsome husband in uniform—a day late—attracted more attention than his absence during the delivery. Once home, there were no offers of help or pre-made dinners to get us through those first few weeks with a new little one under the roof. And when my husband was back on a plane to Guantanamo almost as quickly as he'd arrived, there was no recognition of the heartbreak his departure left in its wake.

That was a decade ago. Since then, we have racked up a handful of deployments under our collective belts. My gang has become fairly savvy about how to live this life of ours. But just because we can soldier on, doesn't mean it's in my family's best interest to do so. Surviving and thriving, especially during a deployment, are two very different things, and the difference between the two starts with me.

I've learned the importance of being proactive rather than reactive. My family's best chances for thriving come when I focus on two key areas—preparing my children and educating their world.

Preparing my children looks different for each child and each deployment. Factors like age, maturity, and individual personality determine how to best meet their needs. For example, when my two youngest children were little, the "where" was very important to them. I put up a shower curtain printed with a world map, and as Daddy moved from place to place we marked where he was on the curtain. For one deployment, Sara would tell folks her Daddy was in "Kansas-tan," because he mobbed out of Fort Riley to Afghanistan. There was a period of time when she was convinced Daddy lived at the airport, because we always seemed to be dropping him off and picking him up there.

My oldest, Katie, values connectivity, so during deployment we orchestrate regular video chats, to provide her with opportunities to update her dad on her daily life.

For all four kids, I've adopted a policy of honesty tempered with "need to know." I share, when operational security permits, where Daddy is, the important job he's doing, and a general idea of when we hope to have him home, while emphasizing that dates are fluid. I answer questions truthfully, even the hard ones.

The hardest question came from Connor when he was about six: "Can Daddy die?" The best answer I could muster at the time was, "You're right that Daddy has a dangerous job. I'm so glad that he's trained to do it so well." Still not sure I nailed that one.

The part I know I get right is letting our children know that I am always there for them, and Daddy is too—even from a world away. In-house we're solid. My kids know with absolute certainty that we have each other's backs. Deployments are tough but manageable.

Preparing my kids also means helping them interact with their world—one which regrettably, isn't as acclimated as we are to the demands of military life or the unique challenges of deployment.

So educating the world my kids live in is another critical part of preparation. When a deployment is on the calendar, the adults who are in regular contact with my munchkins know about it very soon after my kids do. My kids tend to want to talk about this kind of thing publicly, so I make sure the grown-ups in their world are prepared for that. I also ensure that those grown-ups know what to expect—one of my children tends to get cranky, while another gets weepy, for example. Each child has a unique approach to deployment, and I explain that to the adults in their world. In a civilian community, these people only know what I tell them.

Unthinking adults can cause tremendous pain when their words aren't sensitive to a situation. My son PJ, a gifted musician, shared with his guidance counselor that he was contemplating joining one of the military bands. Her response to him was, "Plot another career course because the military is a job for stupid people and you're too talented for that." An elementary school teacher told Connor that if his Daddy really loved him, he wouldn't keep leaving him to deploy. Even I have been on the receiving end of a verbal attack. Shortly after I received word that my husband had been in an improvised explosive attack in Afghanistan, my neighbor across the street—a woman I'd considered a friend for many years—responded with, "Well, we shouldn't be there in the first place."

I stood there in stunned silence. How can I expect my children to feel and respond to situations like these? Our family's method of combating ignorance and inconsideration has been to talk to civilians about what it means to be a military family and also to develop some thick skin. There will always be some who value their own opinions more than they value the feelings of our military family.

Prepared kids are resilient ones, and mine never cease to amaze me. The whole brood of them, in spite of the challenges of this life—perhaps in part because of them—are compassionate and well-adjusted. They're quick to defend each other and our military life against the slings and arrows of those who don't know better.

When my daughter Sara was about seven, we encountered an adult who ranted and raved that our involvement in Afghanistan was wrong and that he was sick of hearing about the need to support our military. I gave him the benefit of the doubt and assumed he didn't know we were a military family. My daughter was standing right there listening, while her daddy was in Afghanistan. I opened my mouth to respond, but before I could say a word, my baby girl said, "My daddy fights so you can have your opinions."

They haven't put "intuitive community members who know what you need and lovingly offer it without asking" on the market just yet. Until they do, if I need help, it's up to me to ask. That's tricky when we live in a military culture that tells you to put on your big girl pants—oh, I mean—encourages you to be as independent and self-sufficient as your soldier.

In addition to preparing the community and preparing my children for deployment, I've added new sentences to my repertoire like, "I can't do this alone," and "I could really use some help." I still cringe a little bit uttering them, but they fall out of my mouth a little easier each time. I've learned that tired, over-extended Mommy is also often impatient-less-than-stellar Mommy. I have a choice. I can be angry and resentful and journey alone or I can enlist assistance. I know which better serves my family.

Randi S. Cairns is the wife of an Army National Guard member and founder of Home Front Hearts. When she's not drinking piña coladas or taking walks in the rain, Randi is busy loving on her four favorite military kids.

Manners Still Matter

Marna Ashburn

*E*tiquette is a word often associated with a bygone military era: the days of white gloves, wives club tea parties, and a hefty book filled with rules for social behavior. Etiquette is sometimes dismissed as an outmoded concept for twenty-first century military families, but good manners are never out of fashion. Good manners are based on the timeless principle of treating everyone with sensitivity and respect.

Good manners are not complicated, and they are not limited to formal situations. I've witnessed many everyday actions that warmed my heart, even on public transportation: a young man who jumped up to give the grey-haired lady his seat on the bus, the gentleman who lifted my large suitcase down the stairs, commuters who kept a total stranger from getting off at the wrong stop. Good manners like these are acts of kindness that keep the machinery of civilized society running smoothly. This kind of etiquette is more important than using the right fork, but table manners make a difference as well.

Years ago when my then-husband was in charge of the Army ROTC department at a university, he suggested we have a social courtesies class for the senior cadets. I thought it was a great idea and I admit a selfish motive. I was eager to spare someone else the embarrassment I suffered as a young adult. Meals at my childhood home were a free-for-all with gallon jugs of milk pouring freely, hot saucepans and wooden spoons on the table, and all of us shoveling food down our throats without tasting it. By the time I finished high school, I'd developed many bad habits. As a freshman in college, I was invited out to dinner with my boyfriend's family and I didn't even know I was supposed to put my napkin in my lap.

Not knowing the ground rules in that situation made me uncomfortable. It was an experience I did not want to repeat. I began to care about good manners, so I observed and questioned those in the know. I even leafed through my aunt's huge *Emily Post's Etiquette* to find important takeaways, like what to do if I have to leave the table during dinner. *Excuse yourself and put your napkin next to your plate.*

Our goal for the working dinner with the cadets was to offer guidance on garden-variety social situations. When you get an invitation, what should you do? *Respond yes or no within forty-eight hours.* After eating at someone's house, do you have to send a thank-you note, or does saying "thank you" as you leave work just as well? *Send a thank you note in the mail, not an email or text.* Which bread plate is mine? *The one to the left.* Which water glass? *On the right.* If you're confused, watch your host or hostess. Eat slowly and think of dinner as a conversation that just happens to include food *but don't talk with your mouth full.*

Our efforts filled a void, because most of the information was new to the cadets, except for a few who'd learned it from their grandmothers. There were a few eye-rolling moments, as if the students were thinking, "I'm a casual person, not stiff and formal."

The cadets soon discovered that knowing etiquette basics was not restrictive but liberating. Knowing what to expect made them more comfortable and confident in any situation. Manners are useful every day, not just in formal settings.

It doesn't matter if, like me, you didn't grow up learning manners like a catechism. Etiquette relies on common sense and kindness more than anything. One basic question of good manners is: "What would I appreciate if I were in their shoes?"

One time I spent the better part of the day getting ready to host two couples for dinner, only to have one of them cancel at the last minute because, as it turned out, they'd gotten a better offer. *If you've responded "Yes," then only emergencies should keep you away. Likewise, if you're going to be late because of unforeseen circumstances, call your host right away, not at the last minute.*

The lessons continue, and I'm still a work-in-progress. From the early days when I carried my drink through a receiving line at a formal event *(find a place to store everything—your drink, wrap, purse, hat—before entering a receiving line),* to more recently when someone at a book signing gently pointed out that our American flag was displayed incorrectly. *The flag should always be hung— whether vertically or horizontally—with the "union" or blue stars in the upper left corner.*

Not too long ago, I realized I'd forgotten to mail a thank-you note for a gift from a friend. Months had gone by. What should I do? *Write it now anyway. Promptness is important but better late than never.*

Then there was the time when a neighbor told me I'd hurt her feelings because they'd had us over for dinner several times, but we hadn't reciprocated. I was a rookie military wife and didn't know better. *Returning hospitality doesn't have to be elaborate. It can be as simple as "Come over for pizza and watch the game."*

Technology often challenges the limits of good manners. In our ultra-connected culture, we face constant interruptions from calls, texts, emails, and social media. Every electronic message is not urgent. Most texts, emails, or calls can wait until the end of a conversation with a living, breathing human being. Swiping through emails during a conversation, or holding up a hand to interrupt a sentence and answer a call sends a message. The message is, "You're less important than whoever is at the other end of my phone." *In general, it's rude to impose a one-sided conversation on others. Step away from the table, group, or waiting line for an absolutely necessary call or text. Find a secluded place and take care of business, then return to friends and family with full attention.*

Etiquette in action broadcasts who we are and what we stand for. White gloves and formal teas may be a thing of the past, but kindness, graciousness, and consideration will help us navigate military life in the present.

Marna Ashburn is an Air Force daughter, former Army wife, and author of several books, including *Household Baggage* (Wyatt-MacKenzie) and *64 Easy Answers About Etiquette for the Modern Military Spouse* (CreateSpace). Marna still blushes at the memory of carrying a drink through a formal receiving line, but has the philosophy, "When I know better, I do better."

Our Roots: Not Deep but Far and Wide

Susan A. Phalen

*W*hen people ask where I'm from, and I say I'm a military brat, they look at me as if I've just insulted myself. This has happened all my life. When I was a kid, other kids gave me the same puzzled look that other adults give me now. I've resigned myself to the fact that they'll never understand. Sometimes, to ease their suffering, I just say, "Nebraska."

My dad served in the Air Force for thirty years. Like most military families, we moved every two to four years. We moved often enough that my sister and I attended a combined eleven different schools before our high school graduations. Some schools we'd attend for several years, and some years we'd attend several schools. As a child it was exciting. As a teenager it was horrible. As an adult, I appreciate and cherish the memories. Life was always an adventure.

The only consistent and stable aspects of my life were my family and the Christmas decorations. Everywhere we moved, we always had the four of us, Team Phalen. And every Christmas, we were comfortably nestled into whatever home we lived in, with the same decorations we'd carried through every move.

As the first order of business in every new home, Mom would defibrillate the chaos by getting the kitchen in order. Once the heart of the house was beating rhythmically, the family could have dinner at the table, and the rest of the house just fell into place.

My folks used varying techniques to get my sister and me engaged in our new neighborhoods. In elementary school, despite our resistance, they signed us up for a softball team at the recreation center. Playing softball turned out to be fun and a great way to make new friends. No matter where we lived, Dad almost always taught adult Sunday school at the chapel, Mom got involved with the women's group, and my sister and I joined the youth group. Again, fast friends were made, and it was all the more convenient that our parents and their parents were friends, too.

One nice thing about moving around a lot was the repeated opportunity to reinvent myself. Basketball at one school, volleyball at another; violin at one school, trumpet at another; a mullet at one school, a ponytail at another. If you were a nerd at the last school, it didn't necessarily mean you'd be a nerd at the next. With every move, there was at least the chance of stumbling into the "cool kid" crowd. To be honest, that never really worked out fully in my favor. That mullet held me back for a while. But there was at least hope and always a new school.

Before I was coordinated enough to do it myself, Mom would blow-dry my hair each morning before school, while I ate peanut butter on toast. We'd talk about things we missed about our old house or old school or old friends, and what we liked about the new ones. She'd lament that my sister and I were growing up too fast, then she'd kiss us goodbye as we ran to the bus stop.

We were never in one place long enough for our roots to go

deep. Our family is more like a palm tree with strong roots that fan out to great distances. We're flexible enough to survive the shifting winds and the occasional typhoon life throws at us.

My dad retired some years ago. Now my parents live in a gated community in Virginia with a strict and tidy homeowners association. In some ways, it has a similar feel to living on a military base, only much nicer. Now rather than spending time stiff-starching his uniforms or working the flight line as an aircraft maintenance officer, Dad enjoys more time with Mom or goes fishing with other retired military guys in the neighborhood.

Over the years, Team Phalen has grown from four to ten. We all live near one another, and though we've been here longer than we've lived anywhere else, we are not deeply rooted. After three decades of military life, our roots still fan far and wide. At no time was this more evident than when my mom was diagnosed with cancer. Weakened from surgery and chemotherapy treatments, she wasn't as strong as she used to be, and she needed more help. So now, when I visit my parents on the weekends, I blow dry what's left of her hair while she eats cereal, and we talk about the places we lived and the incredible experiences we had moving around.

Throughout the chemotherapy and radiation treatments, it became more and more apparent that while our support structure was strong, it was not local. Mom doesn't have neighbor ladies she's known for thirty years coming by to drop off casseroles of love and support, to compare knitting patterns, or play "remember when" over coffee. New friends and wonderful neighbors are supportive, but when a storm like this hits, there's something comforting about being with people who know your history.

My sister and I pulled a page from our parents' old playbook and helped our parents rediscover the network of friends they created in their military life. Despite Mom's resistance to technology, we opened a Facebook group page for her and included as many old friends as we could find, friends we had made throughout the years from all over the world. And much like when they signed us up for that softball team, the Team Phalen Facebook page has turned out to be a fun experience and a great way for them to reconnect with old friends.

My mom enjoys reading the cheerful comments from the friends we were stationed with in Hawaii, or friends she met at church thirty years ago. For her, it's been a bit like the front porch of her far-flung life, where friends drop by with love and good wishes and to play "remember when."

Military families know what it's like to be homesick for something that no longer exists. Once the movers drive away with everything you own packed tightly in that truck, the life you had in that home is over. Sometimes the only way to go back for a visit is to close your eyes and remember.

I remember going with friends to see movies at the theater on base, anxiously seated and awaiting the big show, then rising, hands over hearts in the darkness as "The Star-Spangled Banner" played before the movie. Once, when we lived at Robins Air Force Base in Georgia, my parents took a bunch of friends and me to the local dollar theater off base to see *Raiders of the Lost Ark*. Apparently the movie reel hadn't arrived on time, so the dollar theater borrowed the reel from the base. We were surprised when "The Star-Spangled Banner" began to play, but we knew what to do. We were even more surprised that in a packed theater we were the only ones who stood. But there we were, in the middle of the crowd, a small group of military brats, standing proudly until every note of our national anthem had played. Everyone else just sat there talking.

I sometimes wonder what it would have been like to grow up in the consistency of one house and still be friends with some of the kids from my kindergarten class. But there are things I gained growing up as a military brat that I wouldn't trade for friends who don't stand up for the national anthem. My family has lifelong friends, even if they don't live nearby. We have roots, and even though they stretch far and wide instead of deep, they give us strength in the storm.

Susan A. Phalen is a grown-up Air Force daughter. She served in the Bush Administration as a senior advisor at the State Department and is currently a senior Congressional aide on Capitol Hill. No matter how grown up she is, Susan will always be a brat at heart.

Orders to Go

Deployment

———————— ... ~ ... ————————

"Leave the gun, take the cannoli."
~ The Godfather

Don't Forget the Kids

Julie LaBelle

O n a brilliant sunny day, my husband banged in through the back door and announced, "I have good news and bad news—which do you want first?" The good news was that we wouldn't be taking a trip I had been dreading. The bad news was that a thirteen-month deployment had saved us from taking it. Oh.

My initial three thoughts were: Me, me, and me. How would I cope? I'd been a single parent before and knew what I was in for—sleepless nights, running on empty, no one to pitch in when I was exhausted or lonely. I started a "panic list" of everything we should get done before he left. Most of it was ridiculous—like cleaning behind the entertainment center, where I'm sure the dust would have happily waited for a year—and a million other small details that I thought would make life easier—for me. We began a whirlwind month of "getting it all done." And then he left.

Years later, a friend asked what I had done to help my kids cope during his absence. I thought long and hard on that question and came up with—nothing really. We did all the normal things you do during deployment—wrote letters, made videos, put a map of the Middle East on the fridge. But my overriding thoughts were: "Kids are resilient," which is often true, and "They'll do just fine," which is not always true.

I'd kept them fed, clothed, read bedtime stories, and the hundreds of other things a decent mother does on a normal day. Why then, did every video of my two-year-old reveal a giant brown eye pressed up against the camera lens and a tiny, whispery voice saying, "Dad, come out of there. It's me, Lauren." In my perpetually distracted state, I didn't get it. Years later, while watching our family videos, I realized she must have spent many months believing her father lived in the camera. How had I missed that?

I began to critically think back on those years and their impact on all three of our children. What could I have done differently?

My oldest, a thirteen-year-old spitfire of a daughter, spun wildly out of control after my husband left. Suddenly, she was sneaking out of the house at night, smoking, and engaging in inappropriate and dangerous behavior. I ran on sheer desperation, putting out fire after fire, searching for her, making frantic phone calls trying to find her. I was so consumed with those day-to-day problems that I never once thought to seek professional help. There it was, under my nose, but I was too exhausted to even formulate the thought. With the vast resources available to military families, I had failed to take full advantage. I also would have alerted her teachers and gained several extra sets of eyes, input, and support.

My middle child, a son aged nine, quietly and calmly began digging holes in the vast wilderness behind our house. It was just him and a shovel that year. Every day, he would race in from school, rush through homework, and then head out to work digging another hole, filling it in, and starting over again. He quietly flew under the radar. What would I have done differently for this small, solitary kid, quietly working alone? I would have found a sport for him. I would have found a male role model, someone who could have provided him with much needed guy-time, away from our otherwise all-female household.

And our two-year-old? She was still in la-la land for the most part, but there were numerous things I could have helped her with. I could have taught her to speak on the phone with her dad before he deployed, so she wouldn't freeze up and refuse when he called later from overseas. If he lived in the video camera, she must have wondered how he could be in the phone, too.

Throughout that deployment, my children put their own spin on how to cope in hardship. In hindsight, I sometimes overlooked avenues of help that might have provided more strength for them. But I also did many things well.

Sometimes it was my own response as a parent: One day, little Miss Adorableness emptied an entire can of shaving cream throughout the house. What I learned from moments like that was to cool down in a public place first, like the front yard. It is so easy to be undone by a toddler on a good day, never mind the hundreds of seemingly endless ones that make up a deployment.

Sometimes it was all about the family time: Riding in our minivan brought out the chatterbox in all three kids. Perhaps it was the lack of eye contact, the neutral ground, the escape from distractions. Whatever the cause, this was my most important time to listen, especially when I could get away with just one child at a time. This is often where their fears, desires, and even secrets came pouring out. And the singing—it's amazing what opens the channels of communication. That minivan hosted many such fun times—the Wednesday night ritual of eating dinner while going through the car wash is a family memory we still talk about.

Yes, hindsight taught me it's important to take a step back even in the challenges of deployment and really assess how each child is coping. It also taught me that a deployment can draw a family closer together and become an integral part of shared memories.

Julie LaBelle is the wife of a Marine veteran and the mother of a Marine. She is a former preschool teacher and a writer and contributor to several books, including *My Dad's Deployment: A Deployment and Reunion Activity Book for Young Children* (Elva Resa) and *Military Life: Stories and Poems for Children* (Elva Resa).

Tale of the Meat Man

Mollie Gross

*I*t all started with a hot Australian, a pocketful of separation pay, and a craving for beef. My husband had been deployed for four months. I had no job at the time, so my daytime activities consisted of trying to forget that my husband was a combat Marine in Iraq. I did this by watching copious amounts of television, finding hobbies to keep me preoccupied, and inviting friends over to my base housing patio to keep the place lively.

The Iraq War was in full swing. I had stopped watching the news, for the sake of my sanity, but steady calls from my in-laws and the repeated horrible news that we had lost another Marine in combat had me on edge. I was not just stressed. I was raw. Honestly, I looked as bad as I felt. I had blown way past the "dependapotamus" stage and was working on becoming something way scarier and stinkier, like the Kraken of Greek mythology. I had been wearing the same outfit for three days: a hand-made muumuu, a byproduct of one of my hobbies gone wrong. I was sitting on the couch watching TV and eating raw cookie dough straight from the tube at two o'clock on a Thursday afternoon, when the doorbell rang.

I looked through the peephole and saw a big hunky man on my doorstep.

"I must be dreaming," I thought. "There are no men left on this base."

But I opened the door without hesitating. Not only was there a man on my front porch, there was a man who could have been Mr. Universe. Any man at this point in the deployment who actually made eye contact with me would have been welcome, but this was a fine specimen. I stood there in the doorway with hair that had not been brushed, let alone washed, for days and a chocolate chip dangling from my upper lip, and gawked at him. Drool slid from my mouth down the front of my shapeless dress.

"G'day Mate! I'm the meat man," he greeted me in accents from Down Under.

I nearly passed out. No man had so much as looked at me in months. It triggered some primitive part of me that had gone into hibernation.

Suddenly, I was running hand in hand with my gorgeous Aussie through the outback—the landscape not the restaurant. A kangaroo leaped by and her tiny baby peeked over its marsupial pouch to wave at me.

My marvelous Meat Man lead me to a blanket on the ground were he had prepared a picnic for me by the edge of a river. He was feeding me Vegemite and crackers while gazing longingly into my chocolate smeared face. He reached up and brushed a rat's nest of hair from my eyes. A sound interrupted us as a crocodile lunged out at me from the water and grabbed a mouthful of one of my voluminous muumuu sleeves. My own personal Crocodile Dundee leapt in to action, brandishing a huge knife, and in one swift move cut my sleeve from the beast's mouth! Dundee jumped on the creature's back and they both disappeared into the river. The water churned as they wrestled, and then it grew still. With a whoosh, my beef-peddling mystery man dramatically resurfaced, shirt drenched, chest heaving, and carrying a pair of crocodile spiked heels and a matching handbag!

"Uh, ma'am? Hello, ma'am?" his deep voice interrupted my daydream. "I was wondering if I could interest you in a meat package?" Still caught up in the vision, I looked at him straight in the eyes said, "You bet you can!"

Five minutes and four hundred dollars later, I had a freezer full of various meats and a lot of explaining to do when my husband saw our diminished bank balance.

The hunky Australian stuck around long enough for me to sign the check, while his five-foot-four-inch balding assistant loaded up the freezer in the garage.

You hear horror stories about these poor Marines whose wives blow all their money on cars or clothes or a new boyfriend when they deploy. Imagine my husband having to explain to his buddies that his wife hadn't left him or spent frivolously on jewelry or relatives, but instead invested hundreds of dollars in frozen packs of meat.

My girlfriends razzed me, too.

"Gosh, Mollie, you're pathetic. A fake accent and a few muscles and you just fell for it hook-line-and-sinker!"

My friend Natalie unleashed on me, "You bought how much meat? You're insane! I guess we all know what you will be bringing to Bunco for the next ten years."

The gossip spread and rumors started. Women snickered and spoke in low tones at the mailbox. I knew what they were saying. I mean eating red meat is associated with a certain level of guilt already, but this was a whole new level of disgrace. I would go back home and cook up yet another sausage in shame and then sigh when I remembered the daydream: the outback, the accent, the matching accessories.

It was so worth it.

Until the stalking started.

Apparently, word got out that the women on base were desperate for male attention and hungry for meat. Or was it the other way around? Anyway, the muscular meat man did his rounds over the whole base and raked in plenty of hungry female customers.

But then the company pulled the old bait-and-switch. Dundee must have gone back Down Under for a walkabout, leaving his less attractive assistant to make house calls. With no accent, no hair, and no broad shoulders to inspire visions, the poor guy looked more like "shrimp on the barbie," from Outback—the restaurant, not the landscape.

I had been their biggest customer, so Barbie stopped by not long after the initial sale. I had a stomach ache from eating too much red meat, and I was deep in buyer's remorse. I shooed him off when he rang my bell, telling him I was still fully stocked and to try back another time. But Barbie would not be defeated. He came back again just two weeks later. Again, I turned him away at the door.

I started to notice he was stopping by the first and fifteenth of every month. Three pay periods later, I was fed up when he knocked yet again, so I refused to answer. I sat as still as possible and tried not to breathe, praying he would just go away. I was exhausted and sick of explaining for the millionth time that I did not need any more meat.

Instead of looking forward to payday as a promise of a spa pedicure and making a dent in my car loan, I began to dread it. All the stress of the deployment and worry for my husband's safety, compounded by this door-to-door harassment had me frazzled. I was down to the last month of Jon's deployment. Not only was I worried about getting my house cleaned and having all the excess hair removed from my body, I was praying to God that Jon would return to me alive and in one piece.

One late afternoon, exhausted after a bout with the Southern California freeway, I pulled into housing just as it was getting dark. My shoes were too tight, I had to pee, and my left butt cheek had gone numb from sitting in traffic. As my home came into sight, my heart lifted, until I saw the meat truck parked in my cul-de-sac.

Barbie was waiting for me. He wanted to corner me out in the open. If I pulled my car in the driveway, he could pull in behind me. I would be trapped. Then I would be forced to look at his meat in front of all my neighbors. The rumors would start up again. He knew that if he caught me in the driveway before I was safe behind my door he could guilt me into another order. I felt so dirty and used.

Barbie knew what my car looked like, and before I could change direction he spotted me and pulled right up in front of my house. The audacity! I whipped a donut and started to drive in the other direction, anything to avoid the humiliation.

I watched the shameless salesman and his truck in my rear view mirror, hoping he would get the point and leave. Instead he started to follow me. I panicked. Where would I go? The events that followed were a blur, and no one really believes me, but this is how I remember them:

It was like a car chase right out of a movie. I hit the gas and burned rubber. I was taking corners on two wheels and blasting through restricted areas meant only for military vehicles. I spun out twice and almost pooped my pants three times. I finally lost Barbie when I drove through a sand box on the playground and kicked up enough dust to obscure his vision. Finally, I got back home, put the garage door down, and was safe behind locked doors. I turned off all the lights and covered my little dogs' mouths with my hands to keep them from yapping. My body was braced against the door like a victim in a horror movie trying to keep out the evil spirits.

It was over. All was still. I heard nothing. Finally, I could breathe. I completely surrendered and slid my body down the door into a heap on the floor and started to cry. Great sobs erupted from my throat, tears spilled from my eyes releasing all the stress, all the fear this cruel stalker had brought into my life.

That's when I heard the knock on the door: "Ma'am, it's me, the Meat Man!"

I froze. Would this nightmare never end? Perhaps because I was so near the edge of hysteria, something snapped. I took a mental step back and looked at the situation: There I was braced on one side of the door, with the protein predator on the other. My chest was heaving, my car missing a wheel. I feared the tiny man with his truck filled with meat and my husband's reaction when he discovered all the crazy food I bought.

So I did the only thing I could do. I laughed. I mean, I really laughed. It was all just so stupid. I refused to cry over this ridiculous situation. It's just meat! Suddenly, I saw it all in the right perspective and broke into unbounded laughter.

The meat man kept knocking, and I kept laughing. It was glorious. Once I saw this for what it was, I knew that no shrimp on the barbie, no amount of stress was going to take away my God-given ability to laugh.

When recalling the event to my two surrogate spouses, Liz and Natalie, on my back patio later that night, we erupted into uncontrolled laughter again. It felt so good to be laughing about it instead of cowering behind my locked door.

"You are probably the only wife on base who ran away from male attention," Natalie teased me.

Liz looked over at me, and said, "Mollie, you saved me on this deployment. You have kept me laughing every day."

My girlfriends and the Meat Man reminded me that laughing at situations that are absurd instead of stressing over them keeps me healthy and sane. By laughing, I owned the stress instead of it owning me. Sometimes when our spouses deploy, we channel our fear and anger into another source so we don't have to face worry.

These circumstances that had been stressing me out were not life and death. My husband was dealing with life and death. On the home front I was safe. I didn't need to introduce any more stress into my life or Jon's by being overly dramatic. I did not need to make my life a war zone. When I put things in perspective, I realized I could use the one tool I had almost forgotten how to use. I could laugh.

Laughter and positive energy are contagious. So is stress. When I was stressed, my husband could pick up on it when he called home. My friends could pick up on it when we hung out. It was time to send out a new energy into my environment.

The laughter healed me. When I passed it on, the laughter healed my friends, and now I hope it heals you, too.

Mollie Gross, wife of a Marine veteran, is a standup comedienne and motivational speaker. She is the author of *Confessions of A Military Wife* (Savas Beatie) and the creator of a comedy CD *Mollie Gross: Military Wife Comedy*. Mollie takes her humor to military spouses in personal appearances around the country and via her popular videos on YouTube. She enjoys telling the story of the Meat Man, but to avoid flashbacks, she has not been to an Outback Steakhouse in seven years.

My Oxygen Mask

Alison Buckholtz

I was on an airplane recently, half-hypnotized by the flight attendant's sing-song incantation of the Boeing 777's safety features, when I heard the familiar refrain: "In the unlikely event of a loss in cabin pressure, yellow oxygen masks will deploy from the ceiling compartment located above you. Pull the mask toward you. Place it over your mouth and nose, and secure with the elastic strap. Breathe normally. Even if the bag does not inflate, please keep in mind that oxygen is flowing. Make sure to secure your own mask before assisting others."

The last phrase, "secure your own mask before assisting others," made me smile. In the past, I'd scoffed at the idea—not just on airplanes, but in life—of taking care of my own needs before those of my two children. This was especially true when they were struggling through their father's deployments and absences. The thought of securing my own metaphorical oxygen supply before attending to theirs seemed purely selfish, the antithesis of a mother's role. I was sure that a good mom always helps her children before she helps herself; after all, I reasoned, if the kids are happy, everyone is happy.

Many of my fellow military spouses played it differently during deployments, never missing a girls' night out or an opportunity to host book club. I figured they were doing what was right for them, but I was sure that my situation was unique. My equation looked something like this: The kids' personalities, plus their relationship with their dad, plus the trauma of a cross-country move, plus the long deployment equaled a dynamic unlike any in the history of the military family. Clearly, I needed to handle things in my own special way.

In other words, I was wrong.

I learned that lesson at a supremely inconvenient time, during one of those deployments where big things start to go south immediately. My Navy husband had just left for a yearlong assignment in Iraq. The children and I moved from Washington state back to a home we owned in suburban Washington, DC, to be near our extended family. My son, Ethan, was six years old and my daughter, Esther, was four. We were all still trying to catch our breath after my husband's previous deployment, from which he had returned exactly a year before he headed to Iraq this time.

The bad-news dominos fell fast. Esther was diagnosed with Lyme disease, and soon afterward she slipped off the monkey bars and broke her wrist. Ethan developed allergies that triggered severe asthma attacks, and visits to the emergency room became a routine part of our lives. He cried every night, missing his dad and his friends out West. Sometimes he awoke from his nightmares screaming.

I kept telling myself this was just a rough patch, resisting the idea that the chain of pain portended any long-term ills. At that point, we weren't even a quarter of the way into the deployment. If I stuck to my usual plan—keeping the kids occupied, devoting myself to their needs—I was certain something would start to go our way.

What else could we do but put one foot in front of the other and march forward? That's what I told family members and friends who, one by one, pulled me aside and said they were worried about me. They could see that I barely slept. I was also gaining weight—stress eating is my specialty—and I was distracted and forgot things easily. But I was quick to defend my "kids first" approach, and I dug in.

"It's like triage," I explained to my brother, who had gently suggested I find a counselor. "You treat the people who need it most, first," I insisted. "The kids need attention more than I do right now. Once they're happy again, I'll be happy." I didn't have any objection to therapy. I just wanted to help my kids get better before I spent any resources on myself. It was a question of timing, I reasoned.

He looked at me skeptically, and started to say something, but I cut him off. "I just need to make sure the kids are okay," I reassured him. "Then I'll focus on me."

Swine flu was epidemic that year, and Ethan caught it early in the season. Picture the usual hideousness of the forty-eight-hour vomit-a-thon, dragging on for two weeks. By the end of the second week, I was so sleep-deprived from caring for him that I fell down the stairs in our house. Though I broke several small bones in my foot, it wasn't diagnosed until a week later, when I finally had a free afternoon to go to the base hospital for X-rays.

Hobbling around in my orthopedic boot, I finally gave myself permission to admit that this deployment was not going to get any better, no matter what brand of good attitude I slapped on it. My practical, reasonable self-talk had not kept away the Lyme disease, the swine flu, or the hairline fractures running through my left foot, which throbbed, tingled, and ached all the time.

I finally gave in to the sadness of it all—starting with the timing of the deployment, which had always seemed ill-conceived and unfair. That's when I put myself first on the triage list and called the therapist's office. I was lucky, because it was a great match, and I trusted her from the first session onward.

Of course, these weekly visits couldn't stop bad things from happening. Later that winter, while wearing my orthopedic boot, I slipped on a patch of black ice. I thought the fifteen stitches over my eye were the worst of it, but the fall also left me with a concussion so severe that the symptoms shadowed me for more than a year. I'm so grateful I already had a therapist in my corner, because experiencing that sort of health crisis during a year on my own was the second scariest thing I've ever had to face—a runner-up to having my first child alone during a previous deployment. My therapist was an important member of the team that got me through it, along with the rest of what fate tossed my way in the months until my husband returned.

Seeing a therapist didn't take away any time or attention from the kids. In fact, it made me a better mother almost immediately, because I had someone to help me think through problems—a sympathetic but objective person who reminded me what was often convenient to forget. Over time, therapy became my oxygen mask.

Once I accepted that I did need to put on my own mask first—not just *before* helping my children, but *in order to* help my children—I was able to breathe new life into a year that ultimately brought our family closer together.

Alison Buckholtz is a Navy wife and the author of *Standing By: The Making of an American Family in a Time of War* (Tarcher/Penguin). Alison was sure that a good mother always helped her children first, until her worst deployment experiences forced her to look out for herself.

Buy More Underwear

Karen Pavlicin-Fragnito

We sat on the bed in our Upper West Side hotel room watching *Family Feud*. There was a whole world to explore in New York City, but this is what my nine-year-old son, Alexander, wanted to do: hang out with Mom in this tiny but cool hotel room and watch TV. He was half watching the show, half reading a book about Jackie Robinson and the Brooklyn Dodgers, biding his time until the main event of the trip: a baseball game at Yankee Stadium.

The game show host continued, "We surveyed 100 men. Top six answers are on the board. Name something you do when you realize you've run out of clean underwear."

"Buy more!" Alexander yelled.

Ding. Good answer!

"I learned that from your workshop, Mom," he said, looking over at me with that "you are the smartest mom in the world" smile I suspected he'd soon outgrow.

At that workshop, a military spouse in the thick of her husband's deployment had asked me point blank: "Can you please just skip ahead to the answers? I need to know the most important thing I should do to keep my sanity in this deployment."

The first thing I thought of was, "Buy more underwear."

"When do you have to do laundry?" I asked her. "When you're

out of clean underwear. So if you buy more underwear, you can do laundry less often and have more time for more important things."

Later that same day at the PX, I recognized another spouse from the workshop. She had several packages of boys' underwear in her cart. She laughed when she saw me and explained that while my underwear-buying advice seemed like a decent idea, her prior-planned purchase was a necessary replenishment after an incident the night before. Her preschooler had decided to cut holes in the backsides of all his underpants, so he wouldn't have to pull them down to poop.

The fine print: depending on the age and personality of your kids, you may want to keep a few extra pairs of their underpants stashed away in case of underwear emergencies.

When my Marine husband died of cancer and I became a single parent, laundry was pretty far down on the list of ways I wanted to spend my time and energy. It was on a hectic school morning—when my son realized at the last minute he had no clean underwear—that I first implemented Operation Buy More Underwear.

Of course, none of this is really about managing laundry. I'd be okay leaving it for a month. Some people prefer to wash a load every morning, others once a week; some teach their kids to wash their own clothes at an early age.

It's also not about what to do if you run out of clean underpants. Rather than wash them or buy more, some people might employ the other answers we heard on *Family Feud*: go without, turn inside out, wear dirty ones, or wear someone else's.

The point is that clean underwear should be the least of your worries. Strategies like having plenty of underwear can simplify your life and give you the freedom to focus on more important matters, such as time with each other.

Karen Pavlicin-Fragnito has always found blessings amidst the challenges of deployment, even on laundry day. She shares her experience with military families around the world through her workshops and books, including *Surviving Deployment* (Elva Resa) and *Life After Deployment: Military Families Share Reunion Stories and Advice* (Elva Resa).

What Strength Looks Like

Angela Caban

When I dropped my husband off at his unit for a fifteen-month deployment, my life changed, not just for the duration of the deployment, but forever. I didn't realize then just how much these experiences would shape us for what we would experience during and after deployment. As an Army National Guard family, our life is different from what some might call traditional military life. We live in a civilian community, a three-hour drive from the nearest military installation. At first I thought it was better that way, but six months into the deployment that thought disappeared, leaving me feeling isolated and anxiously searching for others like me.

Before we were married and before he joined the National Guard, my husband, Vincent, was an active duty single soldier for eight years and lived on a military installation. After getting married and joining the guard, he had to learn a new way of living military life, with a family in a civilian community. Military life isn't only about the service member. Support for the family is an important piece of military life, but at first my husband didn't know much about that. I didn't know much about the military at all, so we both had a lot to learn about this new life.

When we were first married, I didn't think the military would play a big role in our lives. I figured one weekend a month and two weeks for training during the summer would be all we signed up for. Things changed rather quickly as temporary duty, training, and deployments made my husband much more than a weekend warrior. Now I was faced with the challenge of learning and accepting the military as part of our life—my life.

When Vincent left for that first deployment, I didn't know what it meant to be a military family. I honestly thought everything would fall into place and the support I needed would be there. Support wasn't automatically there, and I learned I had to search for it. I also found out I had to search for my own strength, but first I had to find out what it meant to be strong.

I didn't want anyone to know that I was struggling, and I put on a very good front, because that was my definition of strong. My work friends were amazed that I had just sent my husband off to war and I wasn't falling apart. I didn't think I needed help, and neither did anyone else. I thought I was capable of managing everything on the home front. No need to tamper with my neatly arranged schedule. If I had any doubts, I hid them, even from myself. The military was not going to change me or my life. Of course, nothing ever stays the same during deployment. It couldn't when a major piece of my life—my husband—was absent.

The first week of his deployment, I was set on continuing life as usual. I thought I was being strong. Then the dishwasher broke down. It didn't only break, it fell out of the wall and flooded my entire kitchen floor. I struggled to push it back into the wall, and the situation went from bad to worse. Water flowed into the living room, where my son was splashing around in dirty dishwater.

Great. It wasn't long before the tears started pouring out. I sat in the middle of the floor crying and asking God why my husband couldn't be here. I was not handling this crisis at all the way I had imagined.

I thought I was strong, but I broke down along with the first household appliance. I didn't want to break, but I had to in order to discover real strength. I wasn't really crying about the dishwasher. I wanted my husband back. I didn't want to go through the next fifteen months alone. Sitting in the middle of my floor, at my weakest point, I began to recognize that I could do some things on my own, but for others I would need help. For starters, I needed professional dishwasher help. That was the beginning of my journey to real strength, not just toughing it out. When I needed help I would have to ask for it. When I needed strength, I would have to find it.

I found a support group online, through a program called Wives of Faith. These were military wives scattered all over the country who shared my military experiences and my faith. I felt validated by the support of other military wives, particularly those who also lived far from military installations. Corresponding with military spouses who were going through the same issues of isolation, sharing our struggles, fears, and personal triumphs was a welcome source of reassurance.

I needed the moral and spiritual support of others in my situation. I also needed physical support of those who lived nearby, my civilian friends and family. I had to learn that asking for help is not weakness. During that deployment, I had family nearby.

To tap into the strength and support they had to offer, I had to admit I needed it. Being strong isn't about holding back tears, and asking for help is not weakness. Strength is daring to cry and then carry on. Strength is recognizing when I need help and not being ashamed to look for it.

Angela Caban is the wife of an Army National Guard member, a writer and speaker, and founder of Homefront United Network. Angela's military life has its twists, turns, and appliance breakdowns, and is guaranteed never to be boring.

Friends in Need, Friends in Deed

Benita Koeman

*O*ur military community becomes a surrogate for our own extended family, which is often far away. Being as close as family doesn't mean we always know what to do to help those who are struggling through a deployment, a loss, or difficult time. We say, "Let me know what I can do," or "Call if you need me," because it feels better than saying nothing. Unfortunately, a family in stress may not know exactly what they do need.

Plan ahead for potential needs and look for opportunities to serve. Anticipate needs. Act without being asked. Look for those in your life who need a simple chore performed, an errand run, or who might need a meal—a new neighbor, a friend, someone you hardly know. These tips and techniques can help your efforts be more effective.

Give without expectations. Giving is not about the giver, it's about the recipient and the need. Give without expecting warm, fuzzy hugs or thank you cards in return. Be patient and sensitive if your offer to help is denied. Make friends, not projects.

Give your time. Giving doesn't have to cost a lot of money. Time is a valuable gift. Offer to babysit or run an errand. Offer prayers. Send an encouraging note. Use words like: "You've been on my mind," "I've been praying for you," "I care and I want to help."

Involve your family. Seek opportunities to encourage others through covert missions. Have your kids rake leaves or shovel snow while the recipient is away. Leave an anonymous card with an encouraging note at the door. Brainstorm with your family about ways you can help.

Everybody eats. Meals are usually welcome during a difficult time. Take a hot meal for now or a freezer meal for later. Take-out meals are also helpful and appreciated, if your culinary skills and time are limited. Ask about dietary restrictions.

Plan ahead for spontaneity. Have a few standard go-to dishes and keep the ingredients on hand so you're ready when the need arises. When baking cookies or preparing a meal, double the recipe and freeze remainders. Then you'll have something to give away, even when you're short on time.

Coordinate with friends and neighbors. This creates a network of care and prevents an abundance of lasagna. Online tools can help coordinate large groups. Connect face to face whenever possible.

Make it easy for the recipient to receive your offer. Be specific. For example, say, "I'm available Tuesday or Thursday afternoon. I'd like to help you by watching your kids. Which day works better for you?" or "I'm making a huge pot of chili tomorrow. Can I bring you some as well?"

Look for people in your life who might be silently struggling. While others are rallying around other needs that are more obvious, be the person who seeks out those who may have fallen through the cracks, those who may not be as connected, or those whose needs are long-term and whose support has dwindled.

Give sacrificially. Yes, it may be inconvenient. Yes, it takes time and energy to help someone else. Remember how much it meant to you when someone helped you, and know that your efforts are appreciated and make a difference.

Benita Koeman is an Army wife and the creator of Operation We Are Here, a clearinghouse for military family resources and information. She was inspired by her own deployment experiences, both good and bad, to help other families have better ones.

Check, Please

Careers & Finances

······ ~ ······

*"When a man's stomach is full,
it makes no difference whether he is rich or poor."
~ Euripides*

Secrets of My Success

Lisa Smith Molinari

*I*t all started about a million years ago, when I had a career, a briefcase, an office, a secretary, and a view from the twenty-fourth floor. I did research, argued motions, interviewed clients, and attended the firm holiday party. My name was on the wall in the lobby.

As I lay my head on the pillow of my twin bed, in my sparsely decorated Pittsburgh apartment, I dreamt of working my way up the ladder, becoming a partner, meeting another local professional, getting married, having children, living in a renovated historic house in an established neighborhood.

Little did I know, the direction that I had carefully planned for my life was about to change. Big time.

It happened one summer, while I was on vacation with my family on the coast of North Carolina. I'd just returned from the beach. My wet hair had fallen into an unflattering middle part, there was sand in my ear, and I was wearing a rather unattractive two-piece bathing suit. I was sitting on the deck of the beach house in an unladylike pose, shucking corn.

"Hey Lisa, this is Francis—a buddy of mine from VAQ-139 at Whidbey Island," my brother said, leading his Navy squadron mate up onto the deck. I looked up from my pile of husks, and it was all over. Through. Finished. Turn me over. Stick a fork in me. Done.

Without the slightest warning, I'd been blindsided by love, and a few years later, I found myself sitting on Francis's old bachelor couch in our tiny base house, in a state that did not recognize my law license, nursing our new baby and watching Maury Povich interview people who'd been abducted by aliens.

But I wasn't concerned. I was pretty much ecstatic to have met such a great guy and to be home with our brand new adorable little baby boy. Although things weren't going exactly according to my plan, I thought naively that I'd still get back to my legal career in the very near future.

In between baby feedings, I fed my dreams of becoming a seasoned litigator. I studied my law updates, did part-time research and writing for local firms, and kept my suits cleaned and ready for interviews.

Another three years went by, and there I was, still sitting on that same old couch—this time stationed in England—nursing a new baby girl, watching *EastEnders*, and crying.

So many unexpected things had happened in those three short years. My father left my mother after thirty-five years of marriage. We got orders to go overseas for three years. We said goodbye to family and friends. We spent a small fortune on the required quarantine for our cat. I had a miscarriage. My husband's grandmother died, and we couldn't afford to go back to the States for the funeral. I got pregnant again. My grandfather died, and again we couldn't afford to attend the funeral. With the help of an Irish midwife, I gave birth to Baby No. 2.

Needless to say, I hadn't gotten back to my legal career yet.

But I wasn't crying about all that. I was crying because my husband and I had just returned from taking Baby No. 1 to a developmental pediatrician at Lakenheath Royal Air Force Base. He told us that our three-year-old son had autism.

The next several months were a whirlwind of controlled panic. After shedding more tears than I thought humanly possible, I made a frantic plan to do whatever it took to make our son well. I read everything I could get my hands on, kept detailed records of everything my son did in a spiral-bound notebook, did daily home play therapy, and got our son involved in every developmental program we could afford.

In the meantime, I tried to bond with Baby No. 2 by keeping her wrapped against my body 24x7 in a soft denim Snugli. The poor thing was breastfed while I wrote in that spiral-bound notebook, I changed her diapers while I showed my son flashcards, and I bathed her while I sang songs with my son.

A few times a week, however, my son went to therapy or preschool for a couple hours. During those precious moments, I'd look into my baby girl's glossy brown eyes, give her 100 percent of my attention, and ask her to forgive me. She always did.

A couple years after moving back to the States and buying our first house, I was nursing Baby No. 3 (and asking for her forgiveness) in the lobby of another therapist's office in Virginia Beach, Virginia, waiting for our son to finish speech therapy, so I could go pick up Baby No. 2 from preschool. I was scribbling notes into the spiral-bound notebook, now dog-eared from frequent use.

The good news was, my son was getting better. Originally

diagnosed by three different doctors with autism, his diagnosis had been downgraded since we started his intensive therapies. We hoped that, if we kept up the hard work, our son could overcome all of his issues.

Of course, during this whirlwind, my husband got deployed, worked watch hours, changed jobs, traveled, and had no choice but to leave me in complete charge of our son's disorder, our girls, our house—essentially, every aspect of our family life.

My legal career was rapidly becoming a distant memory.

At that point in my life, I barely had time to brush my hair, much less attend to my professional interests. In fact, as soon as we found out our son needed help for his developmental issues, I stored my law books in cardboard boxes and gave my suits to the Salvation Army. My resume, transcripts, writing samples, and license documents were relegated to the neglected bottom drawer of our filing cabinet.

I had more important things to do.

My days were an intense flurry of toaster waffles, home play therapy, baby wipes, sensory integration therapy, birthday parties, house cleaning, speech therapy, chicken tenders, marble jars, yard work, physical therapy, Halloween costumes, doctor appointments, individualized education program meetings, jogging strollers, gluten-free-casein-free diets, potty training, and boo-boo bunnies.

If I didn't have enough to do, I religiously kept a log of my son's daily life in the well-worn spiral-bound notebook, chronicling therapies, activities, play, sleep, speech, meltdowns, food consumption, breakthroughs, and setbacks.

Eventually, all that seemingly masochistic hard work started paying off: our son made outstanding progress, ultimately losing any autism spectrum diagnosis and becoming a "normal," albeit quirky, fifth-grade boy. Although our son tested out of all the therapies and no longer needed specialized education or a special diet, I still tried to help him with some lagging social awkwardness and speech idiosyncrasies.

All three kids were in school, and my husband was home. Was it finally time for me to restart my legal career?

After so many years of dedicating myself to my family at the expense of my own career aspirations, my emotions were mixed.

First of all, it had been more than a decade since I had practiced law, and my work experience was outdated.

Second, I realized that I would have to take the bar exam again to get licensed in Virginia. And I wouldn't have a chance of passing unless I took an extensive bar exam review course. Where would we find the money? What if I failed? Even if I passed, who would hire me? If someone were willing to hire me, how would I be able to commit to full- or even part-time work now that my family relied on me being at home? What if I succeeded and got a job—right before we got orders to move somewhere else?

I finally overcame my misgivings and started rehearsing my potential interview in the shower. Then my husband received orders for a yearlong remote assignment to Djibouti.

That was it. The tiny ember I hoped would one day rekindle my legal career was doused by a deluge of military reality. Once again, there was no time to consider my career goals; my family still needed me.

Soon after waving at the plane that took my husband across the Atlantic Ocean, I was back at it, managing our home life and all that came with it.

A few years later, I was having an argument with my son in our stairwell-housing apartment, on Patch Army Barracks in Stuttgart, Germany. At fifteen, he had decided I was his enemy. Except when he needed food, allowance, birthday presents, clean laundry, and all-night pizza parties with his friends, I was to be avoided at all costs.

Like other parent-teen rows, it went round and round, in illogically argumentative circles, spewing unfortunate words, but getting nowhere. The girls were used to it, having learned that all teenage boys are icky anyway. My husband, tired and hungry, unbuttoning his blueberry fatigues from another stressful workday, didn't want to deal with it.

I don't recall what sparked this particular mother-son argument, but I will never forget my husband's reaction.

"Stop being disrespectful to your mother!" he suddenly boomed, entering the room where my son and I stood toe to toe.

"I know you think there is nothing you don't already know, but do you have any idea what your mother has sacrificed to give you a better life? You might think that your parents are idiots, but do you even know that your mother is a lawyer?"

Our son, in the midst of mustering another eye roll, suddenly looked surprised. "Uh, well, I guess, but … "

My husband, who would have much preferred to hit the Barcalounger and watch *Seinfeld* reruns while I dealt with the kids, decided that this time, he would set the record straight. For twenty minutes, he told our son about my career as a litigation attorney, about military moves, about developmental issues, about special diets, about home therapy, about doctor appointments, about spiral-bound notebooks, about how his mother put her own aspirations aside to dedicate herself to handling the demands of military life and motherhood.

My husband's harangue was powerful—maybe not enough to permanently quell our son's teenage angst—but powerful enough to spark a change in my own skewed perspective.

Hearing my husband articulate what I had been doing with my life over the course of the last seventeen years, I realized that "military spouse" is not just a flat descriptive term of someone who is married to a service member.

It finally dawned on me that being a military spouse was not merely another identifying term, like "brown eyes" or "Caucasian" that could be used to describe me on a form at the DMV.

No, being a military spouse was a thing, a real thing.

Despite the challenges I'd faced in our military life, I had always thought of myself as an attorney who failed to manage my family responsibilities well enough to attend to my career. I was blind to the fact that I had not failed. Quite the contrary, I had used the determination and strength I needed to become an attorney to take on the extraordinary challenges of being a military spouse and mother of a special needs child.

Like a career, a calling, a profession, a passion, a life's work—being a military spouse takes complete commitment to a demanding lifestyle that requires strength, intelligence, courage, and resourcefulness. My husband's words gave me a newfound perspective, to stop feeling guilty about putting my legal career aside and start being proud of the hard work and sacrifices I'd made over the years.

I've been a stay-at-home military spouse for more than two decades now with no more regrets. Instead, I'm brimming with sappy, corny, patriotic military pride. Our son wrote his college application essay about the unique challenges he faced as a military child. I'm proud of him, too.

The old hanging folders in the bottom drawer of our filing cabinet contain the only tangible evidence of my career as a litigation attorney. Now yellowed and stained with spots of rust from ancient paper clips and staples, they'll never supplement any future application for my employment. But, I won't throw them away. They are part of our history, the foundation of my essential role in our family.

The file drawers above contain my children's birth certificates, report cards, physical forms, the deed to our first house, mortgage documents, college savings statements, the dog's shot records, orthodontist bills, car insurance policies, passports, tax forms and, yes, that tattered spiral-bound notebook. The documentary evidence of two decades of military life.

I may have given up some dreams to dedicate all my time to

handling the special needs of my military family, but I didn't give up success. On the contrary, I found out that the successes of life could be sweeter than I had ever imagined.

Lisa Smith Molinari is a Navy wife and writer of the syndicated column "Meat & Potatoes of Life." Her writing has appeared in many publications, including *The Washington Post*. Her law career might be ancient history, but Lisa's adventurous military life will never grow old.

Having It All

Tanya Biank

a can of Campbell's SpongeBob SquarePants soup showcased my maternal shortcomings. One evening my five-year-old son, Jack, bounced into the kitchen at our home on Carlisle Barracks, Pennsylvania, rummaged through a bottom shelf, and with both hands, clasped the soup like a chalice.

"I think I'll have this for dinner!" he announced, quite happy with his selection. I checked my watch and my heart sank.

It was after 7:00 p.m. Not only hadn't I thought to feed Jack, but he had clearly become comfortable looking after his own dietary needs while I toiled away at my desk a half-step ahead of a looming book deadline. I'd become adept at typing with one hand and cradling Jack's newborn sister, Violet, in the other. Jack was apparently learning to take care of himself.

After having a miscarriage during my husband's deployment to Iraq, finding out I was pregnant with Violet was welcome and joyful news. The only glitch- -a month earlier I'd signed a contract to write a 100,000-word manuscript with a twelve-month due date.

Our family was also moving that summer. I didn't need to be a math whiz to figure out this timeline was going to equal a real mess.

"When can she deliver?" my book editor back in New York wanted to know. Not the baby, but the book. In the end I did birth both. The resulting mixture of joy, fear, and stress taught me that I couldn't have all, be all, and do all—at least not all at the same time.

SpongeBob, the little bugger, reminded me of that.

So why do so many military spouses try anyway? It's a character trait with a long history. Just look at those military wives on the frontier from well-to-do families back East who left comfortable lives and set out in wagons packed with their silver and china to take on a dangerous, dusty, and unknown world.

Their plight makes today's challenges of juggling volunteer work, school, career, kids, deployments, and PCS moves seem a little more manageable.

I've always been inspired by creative, energetic, and multitasking military spouses who realize whatever hard choices they make, there will be gains as well as sacrifices.

In a radio interview, I was asked how I wanted to be remembered. The question—usually reserved for celebrities in their twilight years, whose obituaries are written in advance—caught me off guard.

I thought for a moment. Then the answer came in like water at high tide: "I'd like to be remembered as a good mom, daughter, wife, and friend."

Being a writer hasn't morphed me into a gourmet cook or a great housekeeper. It has provided a kind of fulfillment I hope helps me be a better person, mother, and spouse.

At a charity event for a women's domestic violence shelter, one of the speakers asked audience members to imagine that everything in their life was taken away—their house, their family and friends, their career, and all their possessions. Then we were to imagine that everything was suddenly given back.

How did we feel? Incredibly grateful and thankful, of course. The exercise was a lesson in focusing on what we have, rather than what we don't.

Can military spouses have it all? Chances are, we already do.

Tanya Biank is an Army wife and the author of *Undaunted: The Real Story of America's Servicewomen in Today's Military* (Penguin/NAL). Her first book, *Army Wives: The Unwritten Code of Military Marriage* (St. Martin's Griffin), was the basis for the Lifetime television network's *Army Wives* series. Tanya recently welcomed the Crock-Pot into her life and banished SpongeBob from her pantry forever.

Smart Money

Adrianna Domingos-Lupher

*D*eath and taxes are supposed to be the only sure things, but in my experience as a military spouse, there are two more sure things: unpredictability and unexpected expenses. Think about how much our family budgets are pulled and twisted with each PCS, TDY, training, deployment, short tour, and activation (or deactivation) order. Talk about flexible budgeting. It's tough enough living life in a constant state of mandatory-adventure. The last place we want to see a surprise is in our budget.

Good planning and a little budget know-how are the best ways to avoid unpleasant financial surprises. So here are a few ideas to keep unpredictability away from your wallet.

Be the boss of your money. If the word "budget" scares you, it's probably because you are not the boss of your money, your money is the boss of you. Money is a tool, and your budget provides the direction you need use that tool correctly.

No matter how much or how little money you have, everybody—yes, everybody—needs a budget. You need to know exactly how much money is coming in, how much money is going out, and where that money is going. If you don't know what you owe on your bills, the due dates, and your interest rates for any loan or credit card balance, you are not controlling your money.

What goes up (when you go overseas) must come down (when you return stateside). Deployments and overseas moves really do a number on family finances. Extra pay, tax exemptions, and other allowances pad your bank account. If you're like most military families, you get comfortable having the extra cash around; but when life goes back to normal, you sit at your dining room table staring at your bills, trying to figure out why the numbers don't add up.

Resist the urge to spend the extra cash when it's there. Of course, overseas assignments and deployments often result in a little extra spending you wouldn't normally include in your budget, but you should try to keep all your spending as close to normal as possible. Just because you have extra cash coming in doesn't mean you have to spend it all. Getting used to little luxuries causes pain later when they are no longer affordable.

Set it aside when you get overpaid. Do not borrow when you get underpaid. Military pay doesn't normally fluctuate a whole heck of a lot. I highly suggest that you and your spouse open and read the Leave and Earnings Statement every single month. After you read it, check your bank balance to make sure you received exactly what your LES says you were paid. If you notice a significant increase or decrease in pay either on your LES or in your bank account, put on your Sherlock hat, open up your latest previous LES, and start investigating your pay.

In the event you got overpaid, figure out exactly how much you got overpaid and immediately transfer that money into a savings account, and do not touch it. I repeat, do not touch it.

Defense Finance and Accounting Services are quick to snatch back overpayment errors. Your next step is for the serving spouse to go immediately to the installation finance and accounting office to notify them of the overpayment and arrange for repayment options.

If you get underpaid, the finance and accounting office is also the place to go to figure out exactly what happened and get the paycheck issue squared away. If you are tight on money, do not under any circumstances seek out a cash advance, payday loan, or title loan. These types of loans have notoriously high interest rates ranging between 240 to 400 annual percentage rate and are very difficult to pay off. Those who take these types of loans find themselves trapped in a cycle of borrowing and repayment. If you need financial assistance, the first best options are service branch aid societies: Air Force Aid Society, Army Emergency Relief, Navy-Marine Corps Relief Society, and Coast Guard Mutual Assistance.

It's important for military spouses to know that a general power of attorney does not grant authority to deal with military pay. If a service member is deployed or unable to handle an issue concerning their military pay or LES, the non-serving spouse must have a power of attorney specifically granting the authority to deal with military pay issues. Military spouses should have both types of powers of attorney.

Keep Mr. Murphy away. Oh, that Mr. Murphy. He's always causing trouble for my military family at the most inconvenient times. Murphy's Law: "If anything can go wrong, it will."

My number one guard against my ever-so-expensive encounters with Mr. Murphy and his law is an emergency savings account. Experts suggest keeping six months' salary in a cash account. An emergency savings account is a constant work in progress. It's essential to financial security to systematically set aside money into an emergency savings account every month. Emergency savings is the key to getting through the rough patches like getting underpaid or an unexpected car repair.

If you can't see it, you can't spend it. This is one of my very favorite money rules. There's nothing in the world that makes money easier to save than never having an opportunity to spend it in the first place. Take advantage of allotments to automatically deposit money directly into a savings account without it ever appearing in your checking account balance.

I especially love applying this out-of-sight-out-of-mind approach to pay raises and promotions. It's fairly easy to figure out how these will impact your income. I challenge you to save a raise before you even see it! You'll thank me later.

Keep it separated when your spouse is away. Maintaining two separate households on one family budget is a big financial challenge. When facing a deployment or other prolonged separation, I highly suggest that you separate your spending accounts to guard against lapses in communication that can result in overspending and accidentally overdrawing your checking accounts by either party.

Before you temporarily go your separate ways, please sit down and discuss your finances. Make sure you know who is responsible for paying what, ensure that all parties are aware of account user IDs and passwords, and confirm that all necessary powers of attorney are granted.

Plan like you won't find a job when you move. As military spouses, we face some pretty tough realities when it comes to maintaining seamless employment with each move. I encourage all dual-income military families to plan to cover their must-have living expenses on one income in the event that the military spouse cannot find employment or secure a position with compensation equal to her or his previous salary.

Save for a rainy day (in Paris). Military life is an adventure. As much as I preach about savings, I also advocate a balance between saving and living. All saving and no fun makes life more than a little dull. Don't feel trapped by the idea of saving. When you're saving for fun, make the savings part fun, too. Set aside a jar or piggy bank specifically for vacation savings and stash away loose change. Try my mom's game of not spending dollar bills. She'd put every loose one dollar bill into our travel piggy bank to save toward our family vacations.

Take this fifty-two-week savings challenge. Each week you set aside an increasing dollar amount that corresponds to each week of the year. The first week you save one dollar, two dollars the next, and so on, until by the fifty-second week of the game you've set aside a total of $1,378 for your family vacation.

You can see the world and enjoy your military life without depleting your bank account. And that is smart.

Adrianna Domingos-Lupher is the creator of *NextGen MilSpouse* online magazine and the managing partner of MSB New Media. An Air Force wife, Adrianna has learned that even though life is unpredictable, she can keep unpredictability away from her wallet with smart money skills.

Dare to Dream

Kathie Hightower

"*I* wouldn't trade my life for any of theirs," I thought, as I boarded the plane in Arizona, headed back to Fort Lewis, Washington. This revelation stopped me in my tracks on the jet way, and the guy behind me bumped into my roll-aboard. "Sorry," I mumbled and scurried forward, my mind swirling.

I'd just spent a fun weekend filled with wine, chocolate, pedicures, late night talk, and laughter with five girlfriends from college, none of them connected to the military in any way except that they know me.

At every reunion before this one, I'd come away feeling "less than."

We all graduated from the University of Virginia and expected to succeed in business or government or something important. My friends fall into the *über*-success category professionally. One is a lawyer, one owns an international advertising business, another has been twice invited to the White House to be honored for her innovative practices as a high school teacher.

Then there was me, a military spouse with a professional life full of starts, stops, big pauses, and really big pauses. Often I felt like a failure, trying to avoid the nagging thought: "What if I hadn't married into the military?"

I'd been in the military myself and chose to get out when Greg and I were getting married, because we were going to be assigned to posts miles apart. We figured I'd get my master's of business administration and have no trouble finding jobs. Well, there were no MBA programs then in rural Alabama, where we were assigned.

I started job-hunting the only way I knew how, by reading want ads. The best job offer I got was as a door-to-door Electrolux vacuum cleaner salesperson, a job I almost took. I was desperate for work, any work, anything to keep me from greeting my husband every night in tears.

I considered myself different from other military spouses. I was a career woman, or at least I wanted to be. I had no interest in going to coffees or volunteering at the thrift shop. I didn't even think of myself as a military spouse back then. That way of thinking kept me isolated, the least effective way to approach life, especially this challenging military life.

Fast forward many years, and I'm in a completely different space, because I opened myself up to the power of what I've come to call, "Dare to Dream Teams," to possibility thinking, and to the incredible diversity and depth of military spouse friendships. I wish I'd learned this sooner. I lost quite a few years to my passive, lonely approach.

My first Dare to Dream Team started after we moved from Virginia to Fort Lewis. There were five of us. We met every two weeks at a local restaurant that provided a free meeting room if we ordered breakfast. We brainstormed for each other, wrote down everyone's dreams and weekly goals, and held each other accountable. We each had to report our progress at every meeting, a bit like weighing in at a Weight Watchers meeting.

Teams create accountability. Although I could justify my procrastination to myself, it wasn't so easy to justify it to other people. Plus, seeing others taking action toward their dreams made me want to do the same.

My team sometimes created extreme measures. One time we all met at Sharon's house, staying with her until she made a difficult phone call she'd been avoiding. We walked door to door with Claire helping her market her new massage practice. Carrie and I took turns going to one another's houses once a week, where all she was allowed to do was paint, and all I was allowed to do was write, no laundry or housecleaning or other procrastination allowed.

Since that time, I've started a dream team with every move, with amazing results. These teams can advance any aspiration. The dreams we've followed have been a mix, from career to parenting to fitness to finances. We work toward holistic dreams so no one gets caught up in obsessing about only one area of life.

My team members have expanded my concept of possibility by suggesting second or third right answers. As military spouses, many of our dreams may seem impossible at a particular assignment or location. That means the obvious approach—the first right answer—might not work. That's where second, third, and higher right answers come into play. Brainstorming with a group can trigger other ideas and solutions.

Too many times we stop with the first solution to a situation. If that one isn't possible, we give up and end up frustrated and angry with the military for moving us in the first place or for sticking us in some godforsaken place. Instead, we can look for other possibilities.

For example, after my close brush with vacuum-cleaner sales, I figured out the work I wanted to do: speaking and writing. I had started conducting seminars, and the Army helpfully sent us to Kansas where three national seminar companies are headquartered. I networked with the National Speakers Association chapter in Kansas, landing an audition with a national seminar company to do programs for them all over the United States. My new business was on its way.

Then we got orders to Germany. The company had no work overseas. In order to market my own seminars to corporations in Germany, I would have to pay German taxes. My business wasn't large enough or mature enough to justify that. I thought I'd have to give up seminar work for three years.

I was disappointed that this seemingly perfect solution to having a career while being a military spouse would have to be put on hold. My first right answer wasn't possible in Germany.

Setting aside my disappointment, I made a point of introducing myself to as many people as I could at a newcomer luncheon in search of members for another Dare to Dream Team. At the luncheon, I talked with an Army spouse who told me about a women's leadership conference in Germany. Proposals for workshop speakers were due that week. Talk about serendipity.

Another new acquaintance told me about the Office of Personnel Management, which provides training workshops to US government offices in Europe. Their headquarters was a two-hour drive from where we lived.

I spent the next three years leading seminars for military spouse groups and military units throughout Europe. I was able to build my skills, material, and reputation, and continue in the field I had almost forsaken. I was able to market myself as an "international speaker," something it might have taken me years to achieve living in the United States. Plus, I got to travel and speak in wonderful places like Garmisch, Germany, and Venice, Italy.

As I met with my college friends for this latest reunion, I found myself excitedly sharing all the experiences I was having as a result of my speaking and writing and the other adventures of our military life. I realized as I talked about it how much I love the process of what I'm doing.

I avoid living my life by comparison. Comparing myself to others is pointless and can be toxic. As my friend Claire says, "You are comparing your inners to their outers." We know our own life in full, with all our blemishes and failures. We only perceive how we think others' lives are.

Over time, I've come to appreciate my life as a whole. I value what I have created in this military life rather than focusing on what wasn't possible.

At our reunion, my college friends talked about this occasional gathering of friends as their only real girlfriend time. One said, "My only girlfriend time is watching *Sex and the City* reruns. They've become my friends," and I saw nods all around. I didn't say anything, but I thankfully acknowledged to myself, "I have lots of girlfriend time," deep friendships fueled by deployments and other challenges of military life.

At the reunion, my college friends talked about trips they hope to take to Europe and other places when they retire. Greg and I have explored our country and other countries in depth, in ways most Americans will never do.

I wouldn't trade my life for any of theirs.

Kathie Hightower is an international speaker, Army veteran, wife of an Army veteran, and coauthor of *Military Spouse Journey: Discover the Possibilities & Live Your Dreams* (Elva Resa) and *1001 Things to Love About Military Life* (Hachette). Kathie travels the world giving workshops that help military spouses follow their dreams.

What's Missing?

Janet I. Farley

*W*hat's a picnic without someone dishing a little dirt? Confession time, then. I used to be envious of spouses who weren't married to someone in uniform and who weren't required to pack up their homes every few years, only to unpack it again somewhere else in the world.

Maybe it's not such a scandalous confession after all. Many military spouses can probably relate.

It's not that I didn't love my soldier and wouldn't follow him to the ends of world. Been there. Done that. Got the t-shirt and proudly earned my thirty-year letter for the jacket. It was the little annoyances in our mobile lifestyle that seemed hardest to overcome.

I didn't want to have to ask another landlord if we could paint the walls something other than white or if we could have a dog in the house. I wanted to watch the same tree in the yard grow from a tiny sprig into a full-grown shade tree. I wanted my family doctor to actually know my family's health history. I thought it would be nice to run into people who knew me when I was growing up and would know my kids when they were growing up, too. These experiences are often missing from military life.

I also wanted a real career and not a series of seemingly disconnected hit-or-miss jobs. For the longest time, I didn't quite get how all the unique pieces were going to fit together or even if they would.

Over time, some of these irritations disappeared. Maybe the movers misplaced them somewhere between Fort Huachuca, Arizona, and Germany, along with the microwave oven, the weight set, and a box of sewing supplies I still hope to find before I die.

My quest for a real career has turned into what I like to call a happy work in progress. The series of seemingly disconnected hit-or-miss jobs were more connected than I thought.

Working an entry-level typist gig in a word processing center, I learned to type pretty darn fast, and that skill has come in handy as a writer.

Being a supply clerk taught me the importance of accountability. It also taught me that I never wanted to do that job again. It was a high stress, sucky job at the time but a valuable experience nonetheless.

Working at a library gave me effective research skills, again a bonus for someone who attempts to make a living with words.

Pushing papers as a secretary for a defense contractor who offered a generous tuition assistance benefit allowed me to complete graduate school debt-free. In the process, I also gained a workplace education about organizational effectiveness, or the lack thereof.

A basic career direction started to emerge, and the jobs began to make more sense: college instructor, counselor, trainer, policy analyst, program manager. Throughout all these jobs, I was always a writer. In the middle of it, I added the best job title of all to the mix—Mom.

A career path, linear or not, is still a path. Mine has taken me on a journey, even when I thought I was going nowhere. The detours are sometimes more educational than the straight roads, and I learned a few things:

- When your idea of the best job isn't available, take the best job you can find. You learn something from every job, even if it is simply that you never want to do that again.
- Be open to something new. You never know when one job will lead you to a new career that gives you even greater joy.
- If you can't find the right job for right now, then create your own.
- Volunteer meaningfully. Non-paid work experience is still work experience, and you gain connection to your community.
- Don't depend on anyone else to mind your career or provide you with opportunities for professional development.
- Genuinely build relationships while networking with others. It makes a positive difference.
- Make a special effort along the way to mentor a new military spouse who may be struggling with career chaos.
- Give yourself permission to change course over time. What matters to you professionally at one point may not matter as much later.

Many of the conflicts of our military life have been resolved over time. We finally scored a landlord who liked dogs and let us choose what color to paint the walls. We became experts about our own healthcare, after communicating our history to so many doctors through the years. We learned to appreciate the beauty and variety of annual flowers in the garden. And as for longstanding relationships, the other day I ran into an old friend and mentor at an awards ceremony on post. She was my boss years ago when I was a newlywed. She gave me a warm hug and asked me how my daughters were doing; she hadn't seen them in a while.

The satisfaction I once thought was missing from my military life isn't missing after all.

Janet I. Farley is the wife of an Army veteran and a career consultant. Her books include *The Military Spouse's Employment Guide* (Impact Publications) and *Quick Military Transition Guide* (JIST Works). Janet has found success by giving good career advice and taking it, too.

With a Little Help From My Friends

Sue Hoppin

*M*aybe it was the aura of desperation wafting off me at the squadron spouses' meeting. Somehow they sensed my weakness. We were stationed at our first operational base in Wichita, Kansas, when my husband left for his first deployment. I was a new wife and a new mom, thousands of miles away from my extended family, and absolutely clueless about the military lifestyle. TDY, DEERS, MTF, and DFAS may as well have been Greek, they were all so foreign to me. My husband and I were the newbies in the squadron, going through our first deployment when everyone else was so much more experienced. I was essentially the girl without a clue. The other spouses could have snubbed me. They could have laughed at my naiveté, but they didn't. They befriended me. They mentored me. Two women in particular, Wendy and Carol, became my support network.

About the time my toddler had me pulling my hair out, they would show up with their own broods in tow, and we'd all be off to a park or the nearest McDonald's with a play area. The kids could work out their excess energy, and the moms could squeeze in some adult conversation. And when I was having a particularly rough night—worried by news reports from the war zone—they didn't mind a 3:00 a.m. call from me. Often they were up anyway, because they'd heard the news, too. We spent holidays together.

When we found out the squadron had been extended for another couple of weeks, we commiserated together. We were never alone if we didn't want to be. I am eternally grateful to these women for their friendship and the lessons they taught me. Over the next three years, Wendy, Carol, and I made it through that deployment and so much more.

Ten years later, after two back-to-back overseas assignments and with my son in school full time, I could think about starting my own career. But, a lot of time had passed since I'd graduated from college or even had time to think about my personal goals. I had no idea where to start. Again, when I was lost, it was a military spouse who came to my rescue and became my mentor. Janet taught me about networking, connecting with like-minded individuals. She showed me how to navigate the culture in Washington DC, where we were stationed. Her guidance and inspiration led me to a dream job with a military nonprofit.

Since then, it's become my mission to connect military spouses, to show them the importance of networking and mentoring. Since my husband's retirement, our moving and deployments are behind us. Inspired by the friends who helped me, I want to continue to reach out to military spouses, to share what I have learned from my years as a military spouse, from those who cared enough to help me out along the way:

- Seek out friends to stand beside you in military life. They will keep you company and keep you sane. Do the same for them.
- Seek out mentors who are ahead of you in military life. They

will guide you, and share their experiences.

- Mentor other spouses along the way. When you gain experience and knowledge, share it.
- Be aware of your resources and benefits. If you don't use them, they will go away.
- Stay aware of what's going on with military benefits and give feedback when asked.
- Get involved. Show up. Develop connections before you need them. The time to meet the other folks in the squadron isn't when you need something from them.

Remember, you are not in this alone. Other military spouses will be your best friends, resources, and advocates. Your family and civilian friends fulfill essential roles in your life. However, they probably won't understand or help navigate the challenges of military life. For that, depend on your military friends and mentors, and then pass it on.

Sue Hoppin is the wife of a retired Air Force officer, the founder and president of the National Military Spouse Network, and the coauthor of *A Family's Guide to the Military for Dummies* (Wiley). A self-proclaimed social introvert, Sue overcame her shyness to get out there and meet new people and realized the value of networking in successfully navigating the military lifestyle.

Coffee & Dessert

Sweets for the Journey

——————————— ... ~ ... ———————————

"Seize the moment.
Remember all those women on the Titanic
who waved off the dessert cart."
~ Erma Bombeck

Always Time for Coffee,
Always Room for Dessert

*T*he stories in this book are just the beginning. You, in your own home, your own circle of friends, and your own community, have many ways to continue the conversation, share your experience, and support one another. We hope you'll begin by always making time for coffee (or a walk) with a friend and always finding room for dessert (or other sweet blessings of military life).

~ *Coffee* ~

Imagine wrapping your fingers around a warm, inviting cup of coffee on a chilly morning, or sipping a cold glass of lemonade in the shade on a hot afternoon, or toasting a special occasion with flutes of champagne on an elegant evening. Time with friends can be comforting, refreshing, or celebratory too, a pick-me-up, a quencher, a pat on the back. Finding the time to cultivate friendship is challenging in a busy and mobile military life, but friends are more than worth the time and effort. *Stories Around the Table* authors offer these suggestions to help you make time for meaningful connections with friends.

- Invite a fellow military spouse to dinner, even if you're just serving pizza or spaghetti. It's not really about the food. It's about connecting.

- It's a fact of life that all dogs must be walked. Instead of going alone, I call a friend or group of friends to walk our dogs or visit the dog park. The pooches enjoy being in their pack, and so do the humans.

- Ask friends to enroll their kids for the same sports team, dance class, or activity time slot that your child is considering. It will give you time to catch up while you wait for the kids.

- Maximize technology. We use Skype, ooVoo, or Facetime to chat with deployed or TDY spouses. These are also avenues for virtual face-to-face time with friends, especially those who live far away.

- I have friends who enjoy theater, so I keep an eye open for high school and local theater productions we can attend together. These plays usually happen on a regular basis, so it's a built-in way of keeping us in touch. Usually, we'll go out for coffee or a glass of wine afterward. I bought a ticket stub album as a record of these wonderful occasions.

- Using hands-free technology, I have some great conversations with select gal pals when I'm commuting around the area for work or family activities.

- Time with friends is often the first thing that gets sacrificed when we're too busy, so I make it a priority. I mark my calendar dates for family commitments, and then I call friends and set one day in the month to get together. Time with friends is crucial to a well-balanced, happy life.

- My friends and I get together every few months for a fashion show. Everyone brings clothes they're ready to donate, and we have a clothing swap. I always leave with something cute to wear, plus the good feeling that comes with being around friends.

- Philosophers talk about the experiencing self and the remembering self; the latter seems only to know how cumbersome it is to arrange time with friends, while the former would hang out all day once she's in a friend's company. As difficult as your remembering self thinks it is to make time with good friends, do it anyway. Your experiencing self will thank you.

- Like many career-minded military spouses, I'm a telecommuter. To make some of my work hours less isolated, I connect with other military spouse telecommuters for a co-work day once a week. We meet at one of our homes or a local coffee shop. It's the perfect way to engage in workplace chatter when you don't have an official workplace.

- I'm always up for getting together with friends at the last minute, but appreciate that most people are busy with demanding work schedules alongside family activities. So in addition to spontaneous get-togethers, I plan ahead and schedule coffee or lunch dates with friends. My spouse and I also like to throw at least one large party each year where we get to see our friends and their spouses together.

- My friends and I set up a daily gathering time at the gym, usually early morning, and whoever can be there shows up. It's funny how we'll show up for our friends when we might not do it for ourselves. New friends and old are welcome. We get exercise and stress relief, and we also brainstorm, solve the world's problems, and laugh, laugh, laugh.

- I use some of my kid-free time to take a walk with a friend. Sure we call it exercise, but it's really an excuse for great company and friendship in the name of a calorie burn.

- At the start of each month, before I print out our family calendar for the frig, I find one morning when I can schedule a "friend date" for an hour.

~ Dessert ~

We all know about the separate dessert compartment. Even if you are full from the meal, you can fit in one bite of that decadent chocolate torte or a spoonful of pistachio ice cream. There is always room in military life for savoring the sweetness, too. To get you started, our authors dish up these sweet joys.

- The first time you and your spouse's eyes meet after a long separation. You lock eyes and feel as if the earth is standing still. Nothing beats that look. It is almost as if you are meeting again for the first time, yet you already have a lifetime of love to bind you.

- When words can't express how you miss your spouse or how tired you are of packing, but you don't need words, because your military friends have been there, done that, too, and will quietly lend a shoulder to get you through it one more time.

- Retreat at the end of the day when they lower the flag. This simple observance never fails to bring a lump to my throat.

- When your child, all of four years old, runs to the porch at 5:00 p.m. and holds her hand on her heart, facing the flag for retreat. You know you've taught her well.

- No matter how many times I've heard it, I always get a little misty when I hear the national anthem.

- When everything is packed out and we're moving cross country or overseas, when we are in this sort of cocoon of just us—our family—no other distractions or commitments, exploring our new world with curiosity and excited expectation for the adventure ahead.

- The clean slate of a new house, arranging our stuff in new interesting ways.

- Reading other military families' homes by looking at their furniture and decorations and finding commonalities. "Oh, you've been stationed in _____! So were we!"

- Being in control of the remote during your spouse's deployments and eating cereal for dinner if you want to while he's away.

- Every birthday, anniversary, holiday, and celebration you get to share with each other as a family.

- The instant community with military spouses everywhere you go.

- An address book full of friends from all across the country and world.

- Military families taking care of each other. Whether it's helping a fellow military family member land a great job or watching my husband pick up the tab for a lone spouse and her kids at a restaurant, paying it forward—and watching others do it too—brings me great joy.

- Sitting out on the patio or porch, sharing a bottle of wine with my neighbors, the friends that the Marine Corps gave me. While our kids are scampering between our homes, we are there connecting with one another and sharing stories. We are the village. We watch each other's children, prepare meals for each other, and support one another when our military member deploys. It's the most amazing, unexpected gift that the military has given me   good neighbors and friends.

- The look on your child's face when Daddy makes it home with plenty of time for dinner, bath time, and a bedtime story.

- I live for those quiet moments when the entire family is together doing something as ordinary as watching a movie.

- There is nothing sweeter than seeing my daughter hold hands with her first friend after a PCS. There is nothing more reassuring than watching my son blend into a sea of children on a playground after his fourth PCS in seven years. The sweetest thing to a military spouse is seeing and feeling the joy of a military child.

- That first homecoming moment when you see and touch your service member in person and know your prayers for safety have been answered.

- Sometimes it's not only about making room for the sweet, but recognizing it made room for itself. Written or meditated upon, it's beneficial to go take a few minutes at the end of the day to remember what went right or unexpectedly well. It might only have lasted a moment, as is often the case. It's important to acknowledge these flashes of joy, laughter, or contentedness in the middle of so many busy, harried hours.

——————————— ··· ~ ··· ———————————